Speaking of God

Other books by Ben Campbell Johnson

Discerning God's Will
Pastoral Spirituality: A Focus for Ministry
Rethinking Evangelism: A Theological Approach
To Will God's Will: Beginning the Journey
To Pray God's Will: Continuing the Journey
An Evangelism Primer: Practical Principles for Congregations

Speaking of God

Evangelism as Initial Spiritual Guidance

Ben Campbell Johnson

Westminster/John Knox Press
Louisville, Kentucky

Book design by Ken Taylor

First edition

Published by Westminster/John Knox Press
Louisville, Kentucky

PRINTED IN THE UNITED STATES OF AMERICA
9 8 7 6 5 4 3 2 1

Library of Congress Cataloging-in-Publication Data

Johnson, Ben Campbell.
Speaking of God : evangelism as initial spiritual guidance / Ben Campbell Johnson. — 1st ed.
p. cm.
Includes bibliographical references.
ISBN 0-664-25200-1

1. Evangelistic work—Philosophy. 2. Spiritual direction.
I. Title.
BV3793.J59 1991 91-3322

Dedicated to
Douglas W. Oldenburg,
esteemed friend
and president of
Columbia Theological Seminary

Contents

Speaking of God

Preface

For the past ten years I have engaged in the work of evangelism for my denomination. Half a decade ago our major task was reclaiming the word "evangelism" from the trash cans of the church. The word evoked negative stereotypical images with which none of my fellow ministers wished to be associated. So the first task in the work of evangelism was to give evangelism theological integrity and ecclesiastical substance. To some extent that task has been effectively begun.

Once recovered as a legitimate task of ministry, the work of evangelism falls into two major categories, corporate and personal. Of course, these two overlap, but the distinction can be made for the sake of emphasis.

In corporate evangelism we engage the church in the holistic, systemic, and systematic task of carrying out the evangelistic mission through the congregation's corporate life.

Personal evangelism, on the other hand, centers on individuals with respect to their faith relationship with Jesus Christ—one person conversing with another about personal faith in Christ. This task occurs in the church through both formal and informal encounters; it also occurs outside the church in both spontaneous and planned conversations.

Early in my work in evangelism I discovered that lay

persons were reluctant to talk about their faith. I assumed ministers were not. However, I discovered that many ministers also have genuine difficulty talking with individuals about personal faith. I do not believe ministers are totally to blame for this problem. Theological education, the tone of the religious culture, and the dominance of the therapeutic in society have combined to obscure the basic task of one person communicating the faith to another.

As a way of tackling clerical fear and feelings of inadequacy, I have fused two disciplines—evangelism and spiritual direction—to provide a fresh image and a new style of faith sharing. If spiritual direction refers to guiding persons on their journey of faith, evangelism is helping them to begin it. The model of the spiritual director offers a positive, attractive way of doing the work of face-to-face evangelization. In the pages that follow, I have spelled out the implications of this conclusion.

I hope these ideas will give all of us two things: permission to talk personally about the faith, and insights into the basic skills necessary for the task. Most of all, I long for the church to recover this basic unity of ministry.

In these introductory remarks I must express my gratitude to my colleagues Doug Hix, John Patton, and Walter Brueggemann for offering valuable suggestions. My appreciation also goes to several classes of students at Columbia Seminary, who gave me the benefit of their critique of these ideas. And I am grateful to Nan Baird Johnson, my wife, who has tirelessly typed and retyped these pages.

B. C. J.

Labor Day, 1990

1

God-Speech: A Crisis in Evangelism

God.

Speech.

God: the divine who is the source and sustainer of all things.

Speech: the communication of thoughts and feelings through spoken words.

God-speech: the communication of thoughts and feelings about the divine source and sustainer of being through spoken words.

Thesis: The lack of art and passion in God-speech has reached a crisis of major proportions in many mainline congregations.

God-speech contrasts with "God-talk," which makes references to God in every conversation. "God-talk" becomes empty, monotonous, and boring. "God-speech," on the other hand, is candid, spontaneous, natural conversation about the presence and activity of the Creator.

Perhaps we can get at the issue best through the experience of one doctoral student. He stood out in the class immediately: he manifested a "presence"; he spoke with candor and obviously exerted leadership in the class. He not only attracted my attention but proved to be a spokesman for others.

In the opening seminar he introduced himself as Frank Reeves, a surname known to large segments of his denomination. He went on to say, "I resigned from a promising job to go to seminary. When I graduated, I expected in ten years to make a mark on the church I served. My ten years are up and I can't see that I've done very much."

His earnest spirit attracted me and stirred both compassion and excitement: compassion for his sense of failure and excitement to see what discoveries he would make in our studies together. In the days that followed we explored the basic unit of communicating the Christian faith—one person sharing with another. Frank listened and participated eagerly.

As we were departing from the second seminar session, Frank made it a point to say, "I went to seminary to learn to speak with persons about God, but I never received any guidance in that aspect of ministry."

As the class progressed, Frank discovered that "speech about God" could become natural and that many members in his congregation were quite eager to speak with their minister about spiritual matters.

Frank Reeves is not the only person who has struggled to speak directly and personally to persons about Jesus Christ; "God-speech" seems to be a difficult if not frightening challenge to many ministers in mainline denominations. A number of experiences have caused this initial suspicion of mine to grow.

In a required course in evangelism for seniors, I asked each one to interview a stranger about his or her faith. Following the interview they were to write a one-page reflection on the experience, stating what they had learned. The initial reaction to the assignment was: "Interview a stranger? I couldn't possibly speak with a stranger." But after the assignment they reported with amazement that strangers were willing, even eager, to speak with them about their ideas of God. I assumed that if a person could initiate a "faith conversation" with a stranger, every other encounter would be easy!

In a doctoral course I asked a dozen ministers who had been in pastorates from five to forty years to interview the "safest" member of their congregation with respect to that person's faith. The room became very still. Finally, one of the ministers said, "I feel too uncomfortable to undertake such a task." Others nodded in agreement.

Let me share just one more illustration that has intensified my conviction about our reluctance to speak of God in a personal manner. After I addressed a group of clergy and laity on the subject of evangelism, a layman approached me. "What you have said about the reluctance of our preachers is right. When lay persons go to their minister to talk about their soul and the minister tries to psychoanalyze them, makes a joke, or changes the subject, they eventually decide they can't talk to the minister about the things of faith that really matter."

If ordained clergy have a reluctancc to speak personally of God, helping laity to speak freely about God will be extremely difficult. The reasons for this strange silence may help us reevaluate the task.

Am I wrong to claim that the God-human relation stands at the center of religious faith? Is not Christian ministry informed by this relationship—how it occurs, how it develops, the demands placed upon believers, the communication of faith to others? If the relation with God stands at the center of ministry, we ministers must speak about God; we are God-speakers. If we do not know the language, grammar, and syntax of "God-speech," we will find this role boring, monotonous, frightening, or hopeless. Should we not explore this God-speech, to learn how to listen to persons speak about God and how to speak about God meaningfully with them?

Above all else, Christians are to express the meaning of their lives in relation to God's love manifest in Jesus Christ. If this expression can be expected of laity, ministers also must be able to speak personally about God and train others to share in the task.

"I Have a Dream"

Like Martin Luther King, Jr., who looked at the oppression of his people and hoped for a better day, I have a dream for the congregations of my denomination and the other mainline denominations. What might our churches look like if we learned the language of God-speech and began to talk with members of our congregations about the God before whom we live and with whom we have to do throughout our lives?

I have a dream that many clergy would have a new set of priorities, which would include helping members of our churches know the love of Christ and to reach out courageously to persons who need his love. Guiding persons into a vital, personal faith would balance our social passion and church administration. The church requires both growth and maintenance.

As a major strategy for providing this guidance, the clergy would select, train, and supervise a large cadre of lay persons as effective spiritual guides. Both the theology of the church as a priesthood of believers and the practical demands on the minister's time require the development of this cadre.

Selecting these persons requires discernment to recognize the gifts that particular laity possess. Their training would include instruction in the basic data of the faith, encouragement of a deepened awareness of the Spirit's presence in their own journey, and supervision in the tasks of spiritual guidance.

While these lay persons would share in the task of guiding others into the faith, they would also model a higher quality of discipleship—intelligent, committed, sensitive, and involved in the mission of the church. Quality reproduces quality; thus the depth of discipleship would improve throughout our congregations.

Can anyone imagine these transformations without recognizing that the congregation would function with greater enthusiasm and effectiveness? The awareness of the living Christ present in the lives of disciples, and the conviction that these disciples participate with Christ in his mission to the world, would release enormous energy. This fiery enthusiasm would become concrete in sacrificial service for Christ.

What has been said about a fresh vision in the clergy and a new vitality in the laity adds up to a new quality of life together. Nothing short of this revitalization in the community of faith can transform the vast majority of mainline congregations from aging institutions to living, dynamic organisms.

A Proposal

The question that remains is how to bridge the gap between the crisis and the dream. How can we learn to speak of God naturally and helpfully? A different model for making the witness will help. Instead of the proclaimer of the gospel or the manipulative, religious salesperson, we suggest the spiritual guide, which is a softer, less aggressive model.

Understanding the role of the spiritual guide requires historical grounding, a theological structure that informs the art of guidance, and an exploration of style. To function effectively, the spiritual guide must have a clear concept of the subject to be guided, as well as a basic knowledge of the various aspects of faith awareness, the role of discernment, the way the God-human connection occurs, and the pitfalls to be avoided.

In the following pages we will explore these issues, along with the kind of church required to support this form of ministry. But before considering a revitalized church, we must examine the influences that have precipitated the present crisis.

How We Got Here

What has brought the church to this strange silence about—even an avoidance of—the most basic task in ministry? Clergy have been victimized by their view of stereotypical "God-talkers," by the culture, by their training, and by the hazards of the profession.

Perhaps ministers as well as laity have veered away from speech about God because of stereotypical images of those who engage in it. If they do not respond to street-corner preachers or Mormon missionaries, they surely reject the notion of rudely intruding into a stranger's life with a question like, "If you died tonight, would you go to heaven?" Have Christians given up "God-speech" because of these corruptions of style?

Not only has the aggressive witness left a bad taste in our mouths, the kind of faith offered has sometimes alienated persons from normal life, resulting in a compartmentalized religious faith. A typical example of this compartmentalization can be seen in the person who recites the creed and prays on Sunday but makes no connection between that experience and the homeless on the streets or painful alienation from a spouse. Perhaps these perversions would be reasons enough to look for new approaches to evangelism, but there are other forces which have robbed us of "God-speech."

For the better part of three decades the professional training of clergy has given little, if any, attention to the task of evangelizing individuals within or outside the church. The work of evangelization has been lost in the broad definition of mission—"evangelism is everything we do." The average minister has tended to believe that the service of worship, teaching, and pastoral care (translated as being with persons in times of crisis) has been enough. Thus no conscious attention has been given to the syntax—the orderly or systematic arrangement of our words—of "God-speech."

Also, we must consider that the pastoral care movement has looked to secular models of psychology for salvation.[1] At one point it seemed a breach of ministerial etiquette to introduce the name of God into a conversation unless it was done by the person in crisis. In an effort to avoid closing the mind and "leaping into the arms of Jesus" as the answer to every problem for which the minister had no solution, the pastoral care movement almost succeeded in excluding all mention of personal faith, prayer, or worship as means of healing. Ministers who have been trained exclusively in the therapeutic approach often have difficulty speaking directly with persons about Christ.

But why did the pastoral care movement take up arms against talk about God? My colleague John Patton suggests that the rejection of "God-talk" was part of a cultural reaction to an empty authoritarian role filled by those clergy who had to translate every conversation into a reference to God because that was their only way of relating. There was a time when ministers knew how to talk only in religious language; today, many have overreacted by excluding it altogether. In place of religious language they have adopted the language of crisis. Patton says, "Pastors must become 'bilingual.' "[2]

As if these factors have not been devastating enough, many leaders in the mainline churches have scuttled problems of personal faith in pursuit of the earth-shaking, history-shaping issues confronting civilization. The effort to stop the use of nuclear arms makes speaking about a personal relationship with God pale in comparison. But social witness can never become a substitute for personal witness. I do not minimize social witness. If we destroy the world, "God-speech" (and any other, for that matter) is a moot issue. While social witness does not contradict, neither does it substitute for personal speech about God.

Add to these diversionary forces the confusion we have had about an adequate model for ministry. We have baptized a model that functions with a "management by objectives" bottom-line mentality. This model establishes the minister as the Chief Executive Officer, who leads the congregation in setting goals, defining objectives, and utilizing effective strategies to make the "church business" run smoothly. A minister CEO can run such a church "organization" with very little knowledge of God and with no personal conversation about God.

Also, a theology which makes suspect every form of religious experience diminishes the importance of faith sharing with individuals. Perhaps this faith perspective explains why we clergy have been deficient in dealing with individuals at the level of experience and in training lay persons in the art. While seeds planted decades ago still bear bitter fruit, a generation has emerged which asks about God, about the presence and experience of the living God. Because of the deficiency in our training and the urgency for learning the necessary skills, must we not become more zealous in finding ways of speaking with persons about God?

The situation in the mainline churches must be seen against the background of a culture that has broken down. With the decline of the mainline churches in the United States,[3] there has been a turn toward individualism.[4] This pervasive individualism, having lost the sense of community and common vision, turns to personal experience as a norm. Unfortunately, many who have rejected their social responsibility have adopted a pluralistic, relativistic view of religious faith that denies ultimacy to any one faith. Does this not confront the church of Christ with an enormous challenge to rediscover its faith and to learn anew the art of speaking of God in relevant contemporary images? This challenge comes at a moment when the majority of leaders stand unprepared to respond to these stringent demands.

At the moment of this pervasive silence of "God-speech," sectarian, nondenominational, charismatic groups have sprung up to fill the void and answer the queries. While many of us may view their efforts as superficial, lacking in theological integrity, or an endorsement of the culture, these groups are speaking to open ears. In their own way they are responding to the Lord's directive, "You shall be my witnesses" (Acts 1:8); as a consequence of their efforts, lay witnesses, Bible study groups, Christian fellowship groups, and vital congregations have multiplied across the nation. This growth occurs while mainline denominations age, shrink, and rationalize the status quo and their own demise. Is it too late for us to reconsider?

While we evaluate the crisis before us, consider yet another possibility. Will our children who have dropped out of church find us mute when they return? Will those who have gone the route of the nondenominational fellowship find their needs permanently met there? Will they not soon ask the larger questions, which demand an application of the faith to the burning issues of our day? Will the liturgy of the charismatic fellowship provide an adequate life structure? Many who have moved away from mainline churches think of themselves as pilgrims on a religious quest; their present commitment to the sectarian fellowship is not final. When these baby-boomer exiles come home—and Jeremiah did promise to bring our children back (see 31:17)—what will they find?

Three groups of persons place a demanding challenge upon us: (1) those who believe but do not belong, who dropped out of the church in the sixties; (2) the searchers, those who have tested the nondenominational fellowships, the fundamentalist congregations, and the ego-centered experience of the New Age Movement or the inwardness of Eastern religion; and (3) persons nurtured in the church without a dynamic experience of God. When the baby boomers return to our churches, they ask serious, straightforward questions about God and how they can be related to God. When the searchers come back from their far-off religious countries, they bring an assortment of spiritual experiences which they want help in sorting out. And perhaps the greatest challenge of all comes from those who have remained in the church but have not yet experienced the transforming power of the gospel. All three groups of persons demand that we learn "God-speech" so that we may effectively fulfill our vocation as "witnesses."

What does the return of the children imply for the mainline churches? Does it not cry out for a church with vitality, with deep sensitivity to God? Must we not have pastors and lay persons who are knowledgeable in their faith and in the art of expressing this faith to others? Must we not be able to help persons relate to God?

For those who object that an emphasis on personal, religious faith degenerates into a sick individualism, I would be willing to defend the thesis that the way forward, in part, is inward. The inwardness of faith does not, in the finest sense, lead to privatization. Rather, the pathway into the depths leads to springs of inspiration and to the water of life that nurtures personal meaning and also inspires visions of a new society and a new world. Christian faith is always personal but never private. Faith is born in community, nurtured in community, and expressed through community. The journey into one's personal depths, the practice of prayer, and the disciplines of meditation and silence strengthen the individual's participation in the community.

These are reasons enough, it seems to me, to search for a fresh way of communicating the faith. Perhaps a new paradigm of communication is required. In this decade of strange silence we clergy must recover our zeal and artistry in guiding persons into a vital faith relationship with Christ, and also in training laity in the task. To recast evangelism in its witnessing and faith-sharing forms, I have turned to the ancient practice of spiritual direction for a model. In a contemporary form, I believe the norm, the style, and the goal of spiritual direction offer a fruitful approach to face-to-face evangelization. To test this hypothesis we will examine the meaning of evangelism and the meaning of spiritual direction to discover the common link that invites this fusion.

Toward an Understanding of Evangelism

Although the word "evangelism" evokes images of the rude intruder, the sawdust trail, and excessive emotionalism, this word still holds promise for the church; its history and depth will not permit us to drop it from our vocabulary. Evangelism, the communication of "good news," will always demand priority in the church's mission. How unfortunate that a word which means "good news" has become associated with the opposite, "bad news." Because of this contamination, we must look at the essential elements in the process of evangelization and search for a new paradigm for this important task of the church.

FIGURE 1.

If we reduce evangelism to its most basic form, we discover three dynamic elements: God, persons, and a medium of communication (see Figure 1). Evangelization occurs when the good news of God, in Christ, is communicated to the consciousness of a person. The interrelationship of these three elements offers a generic definition of evangelism—the encounter of God with a person through a medium.

These polar aspects of evangelism—God and humanity—can be elaborated in a variety of ways. For example, from the divine pole different aspects of God's nature may become good news according to the circumstances: the emphasis may fall on God's love, God's presence, God's forgiveness, or God's providence. For example, a woman visits the minister with a confession of failure with her daughter; good news for her comes in the form of forgiveness. Or, as another example, good news for a bereaved husband comes in the form of the assurance of God's presence.

Persons being evangelized will vary in their knowledge of God, their motivation for searching for God, and their circumstances in life. The means by which good news comes to human consciousness are as numerous as the creativity and novelty of Christian communicators—the worshiping congregation, the Bible, nature, and memory, to name a few. But in all these polar combinations one thing remains constant, the divine presence impacting human consciousness.

The transformation of human consciousness by an engagement with the living God stands at the heart of evangelism: that is, the conscious experience of God. Meeting God goes beyond mere verbal assent, the recitation of salvation formulas, or empty participation in ritualistic worship; it involves the whole person—cognition, affection, and behavior. This grasp of God upon the whole person creates a relationship in consciousness between God and the person.

The manner in which this consciousness occurs may be dramatic and sudden or it may progress over a period of months or even years. Yet when this relationship has been established, it is not so inconsequential that the subject has no awareness of it. Evangelization refers to the process by which this divine-human relationship is created. Personal evangelism, one way of establishing this relationship, points to the role of one person aiding another in being initiated into a relationship with God.

FIGURE 2.

While the God-person polarity stands at the center of the evangelistic task, two other elements should also be considered. The communication of the message always occurs in a **context** (see Figure 2). This may be anything from a casual conversation over lunch to a worship service on Christmas Eve. Whenever the communication takes place, it is always conditioned by the context. A sermon preached from the pulpit is quite different from a quiet conversation over lunch.

A further element in this generic definition of evangelism includes the human **response.** When the Spirit of God impacts human consciousness, this awareness invites decision. Whether or not to entrust oneself to God poses the fundamental issue: will the individual say "yes" to God's intention? Of course, the appropriate response to this gracious presence of God comes in the form of trust.

We can now state our generic definition of evangelism: **"Evangelism is God's communication of godself to human consciousness through a medium in a particular context which demands a response of trust from the person."**

This generic definition of evangelism still leaves us with

the question of model, or style. The negative style, which has stuck in the memories of so many of us, includes the aggressive witness who, often in good faith, inquires of strangers whether or not they are saved. When the subject answers in the negative, or with a degree of uncertainty, the witness unloads a stock formation of the gospel and asks the person to believe in Christ. Without denying that God has used this approach in the conversion of many, I believe the lack of alternatives to this type of personal evangelism has left numerous pastors and lay persons without an appropriate style and, in many instances, with a disdain for person-to-person evangelism. As a consequence, too many pastors and lay leaders in our churches take no delight in introducing persons to Christ.

Over against this abrupt, sometimes rude, hit-and-run model we need a new style for evangelism, one that respects persons, takes seriously their personal histories, offers an extended relation, and faithfully bespeaks the gospel in ways appropriate to the context. These requirements underlie our turning to the spiritual director model.

Spiritual Direction as a Model

At first impulse the idea of "spiritual direction" may create as negative a reaction as "witness" or "evangelist." The mention of the role of a spiritual director suggests to many the authoritative priest or religious mentor telling another what to do or not do. Were this the role of a spiritual director or guide, we would have made no advance. But modern practitioners of spiritual direction strongly renounce a dictatorial role in telling persons what to believe or do. An examination of various definitions of spiritual direction will further amplify this nonauthoritarian method of spiritual guidance.

Henri Nouwen defines spiritual direction as an art: "It is helping a person to discern the movements of the Holy Spirit in one's life, assisting in the difficult task of obedience to these movements, and offering support in the crucial life decisions that our faithfulness requires."[5] Thus spiritual direction is the work of an artist, not a mechanic. An artist works with intuition and imagination, is often spontaneous, and calls into being new creations. What a powerful image for an evangelist! If spiritual direction is an art, it requires training, discipline, and practice. The necessary training relates to the work of God's Spirit in the soul. Without this spiritual sensitivity, the director cannot discern the evidence of the divine presence. Not only do directors help other persons to discern the divine presence, they assist them in sorting out their response to the Spirit. The art of guidance also includes support. This definition leads to other questions about how the relationship begins and how it functions.

In the best sense, the spiritual director seeks to help a person become more deeply aware of and responsive to God. In most instances, the directee initiates the relationship. William A. Barry and William J. Connolly define spiritual direction as "help given by one Christian to another which enables that person to pay attention to God's personal communication to him or her, to respond to this personally communicating God, to grow in intimacy with this God, and to live out the consequences of the relationship."[6] These tasks seem to fit well with that of an evangelist. An evangelist presupposes the active presence of a personally communicating God in every person's life. To begin a life of faith, this person must pay attention to this action of God. Furthermore, he or she must respond to God's action in faith. The task of evangelization can never be complete without discipleship, which includes growth and change of lifestyle. Thus it appears that these roles of the spiritual director fit neatly with the tasks of evangelism.

Another writer on spiritual direction, Morton Kelsey, states, "Spiritual guidance is the conscious and deliberate attempt to accompany other people on their journeys to and in God."[7] Kelsey picks up on three important elements relevant to our effort. He emphasizes that guidance is a conscious and deliberate effort; it does not occur accidentally. He suggests that we accompany persons; we do not speak from a distance, nor do we initiate persons into the faith and then leave them. And, he emphasizes that guidance begins before persons know God and continues after they have begun to know who God is. All these requirements apply directly to the task of evangelism and suggest the kind of soft, sensitive approach appropriate for many pastors and lay persons.

Kenneth Leech gives spiritual direction a slightly different focus: "It is the process of maturing which sums up spiritual direction."[8] By maturing, Leech means the discernment of God's will and the response to it in all of one's life.

Now what has spiritual direction to do with evangelism? Examine the ways in which these two disciplines overlap. If we should label personal evangelism as "initial  spiritual direction," would not that connect the two? Both concern the divine-human relation: evangelism seeks to initiate it and spiritual direction to mature it. Both deal with human consciousness: evangelism seeks to create a new center in human awareness (the presence of Christ), and spiritual direction endeavors to expand that awareness. Both evangelism and spiritual direction expect a response of trust from the subject: evangelism calls for an initial response of faith in Christ as Savior and Lord, and spiritual direction a continued disposition of trust in Christ's activity in one's life. The focus on consciousness, the creation of a relationship, and the expectation of a response suggest a sufficient connection between these two disciplines to ensure that the style of one will perhaps hold possibilities for the style of the other.

Even at first glance, the style and the approach of the spiritual director seem full of implications for the evangelistic task. The spiritual director engages the person not as an alien but as a fellow citizen, not as an outsider, but as a brother or sister. The goal of spiritual direction aims not so much for one person to change another as for the director to help the directee notice the movement of God in his or her life. The relationship of the director to the directee requires "seeking with" rather than "acting upon"; both evangelization and spiritual direction seek to discern the presence of God in a person's life, rather than to impose a predigested formula of religious truth.

Does not each of these aspects of the director-directee relationship offer a fresh, creative style of evangelism? Christian believers must approach those outside the faith as brothers and sisters, persons whose lives resemble their own more than they contrast with them. The goal in approaching them does not focus on change but on helping them become aware of God's presence in their lives and responsive to it, an awareness and receptivity that has enormous transformative power. In this relation, the Christian witness stands beside the brother and sister, not above them. The evangelist has more interest in listening to a narrative than in face-to-face preachment. While this interest does not preclude the witness of the evangelist and the use of scripture, these may not be the initial tasks. Do not these similarities inspire an approach to evangelism in which most ministers and laity could enthusiastically participate?

In setting forth the similarities of evangelism and spiritual direction, and the fruitful possibilities that the style of the spiritual director holds for personal evangelism, the contrasts should not be forgotten. Spiritual direction aims at the transformation of the subject's whole life in accordance with the will of God; evangelism aims to initiate a person into this process. Spiritual direction presupposes that the subject has a degree of spiritual awareness; the subject in evangelism may be totally unaware of God. Spiritual direction begins when a person requests help in spiritual growth or a relationship with God; evangelism may occur at the initiative of the subject, but most often the witness takes the initiative. In the relationship of direction, a spiritual director will, in most instances, be more passive than the evangelist. Finally, a spiritual director requires maturity and perhaps years of training to be effective; the evangelist can begin much earlier and be of genuine assistance to others in the early stages of the Christian life.

Vision for This Style

If the role of spiritual director were adopted for evangelism, what consequences would that have for the church? Would not this style be attractive to ministers who have never considered themselves evangelists or evangelistic? Does not every minister, at some level of his or her being, know that introducing persons to personal faith lies at the heart of Christian ministry? And if these ministers were offered an intelligent, practical model, would they not be tempted at least to explore it?

What has been said about inadequate training still holds. Today's ministers receive excellent training in the classical disciplines, but they usually lack direction in their own spiritual formation, and they lack the skills to form the spiritual life of members of the body of Christ.

If ministers begin to think of themselves as spiritual guides, many implications for other aspects of ministry spring forth. First of all, the repulsive image of the rude, intrusive soul saver gives way to an intelligent, sensitive, caring, compassionate human being helping persons find the meaning of their lives. This new style will, of course, demand that ministers reflect on their own journeys with God and become self-conscious about God's ways in their own lives.

This image of evangelization lifts the task out of the barrel of cheap trickery and gimmicks and places it on a par with the other essential disciplines of professional ministry. Ministers need not—indeed, should not—sacrifice their critical interpretive skills, their contemporary theology, or their pastoral education to become effective spiritual guides. All these skills still serve the basic task of guiding persons into a vital faith.

Evangelism as spiritual guidance demands that we meet persons in the context of their lives, take seriously their needs and questions, and enable them to respond consciously to God in their particular context. This style contrasts with the use of a prescribed formula for everyone, or the demand that a person learn a new language and liturgy before being initiated into the faith. This style also maintains continuity with God's action in the whole of one's personal history.

Ministers who have begun to develop themselves as spiritual guides will be prepared to meet the "children" when they "come back." Our children who have dropped out of organized religion, or have gone the nondenominational route, will return from the land of captivity. Jeremiah offers us a word of promise:

> Thus says the LORD:
> "Keep your voice from weeping,
> and your eyes from tears;
> for your work shall be rewarded,
> says the LORD,
> and they shall come back from the
> land of the enemy.
> There is hope for your future,
> says the LORD,
> and your children shall come
> back to their own country."
>
> Jeremiah 31:16–17

When the children return, they must find a community of faith alive with the divine presence. If they do not find this vital community they will become dropouts a second time, and the second time will be worse. Those pilgrims who return from the nondemoninational charismatic communions will expect to find structure, liturgy, and accountability. Those who return from no church experience will demand an authentic experience of God. In both instances, the clergy as spiritual guides will be prepared to respond positively to their hopes.

As the minister embraces the role of spiritual guide, the numbers of spiritually aware persons will multiply and the corporate life of the congregation will begin to be transformed through their prayers, their presence, and their service. At this point, a crisis will occur. The professional minister cannot provide all the guidance and companionship required. The minister, therefore, must begin to select and train a cadre of lay members in the task of initial spiritual guidance.

Everything we have said about evangelism as spiritual direction applies as much to laity as to clergy. The image, the style, and the quality commend the task of spiritual guidance to laity. As this shift occurs in clergy and laity, we can expect to see a transformation in mainline churches as the twenty-first century begins to dawn.

2

The Spiritual Guide Through the Ages

Having set forth the rationale for a re-visioning of the evangelistic task and the positive consequences of taking this vision seriously, we must now look more deeply into the role of the spiritual director through the ages if it is to be formative for the evangelistic task.

In a world shattered by the loss of a common vision of reality and slivered into a thousand forms of individualism, one may honestly ask, What can one person do to assist another in becoming aware of and knowing the Almighty God? Not only are we doubtful about the possibility of communicating the faith in a broken world, we suffer greater hesitation at the thought of intruding into another's privacy—especially in the domain of personal faith. Perhaps the very brokenness of our age severs us from the traditions that contain part of the answer. Yet in the midst of this hesitancy to speak, the poet says,

> All that we do is
>   touched with mystery, yet we remain
> On the shore of what we know.[1]

The Mystery of Being

To be human is to be surrounded with mystery, a mystery unknown to other creatures because they do not rise above the immediate to anticipate what is yet to be; neither do they recall in rational form what has gone before. Human consciousness sometimes appears like a wilderness bounded by the ocean of origin on the one side and the great river which resists our march to fulfillment on the other.

Urban Holmes writes about the metaphor of the ocean and the wilderness.

Metaphor

Imagine the land bordering the ocean where the waves crash upon the shore with enormous energy, eroding the soil and filling the air with its noise. Unevenly the shore meets the ocean with its steep cliffs, flat beaches, and long winding fjords.

Beyond the shore lies the countryside. It is a wilderness that stretches back from the ocean and slopes upward toward mountainous heights. Those who would explore this wilderness find the trek threatening but challenging. As brave souls scale the heights they find plateaus with green grass and cool water to slake the thirst of their climb.

Poisonous snakes and man-eating tigers inhabit the wilderness, along with colorful birds and graceful antelopes. Dangerous foes often attack without warning, yet along the way the explorer finds caves for refuge.

The air has a light quality as well as a feeling of eeriness. Travelers are torn by conflicting feelings, which oscillate between lonesome terror and a delicious humor. Even as the journey lengthens by traveling inward, the conflicts do not disappear.

The path to the west, which the lone traveler takes, soon joins with other paths, which produce a band of travelers. On the path now are different kinds of travelers who speak other languages and adorn themselves with different clothes. On the journey they entertain themselves with stories about the depths of the ocean from which they have come and the land of safety and fulfillment they hope to find.

As the travelers continue together they come to a great river. On the other side of this broad expanse of water they can see the land of promise. Although they glimpse it, they do not know how to cross the river and get into the land.

If they are to make the crossing they will need a guide, someone who can point them to the location of a bridge or offer to carry them over in Christopher-like fashion.[2]

This allegory speaks of human consciousness and of that unfathomable depth of unconsciousness from which it has arisen. In that depth, chaos reigns and seeks to engulf the tiny clearing of awareness like a wild animal that lies in wait to attack unannounced.

Between the chaos of the ocean and the fulfillment lying beyond the river there is a bridge that has been prepared by Another. To find the bridge from the wilderness to the promised land we need a guide—someone who knows the way, who has crossed it before, and who can help the sojourner. Holmes suggests that this person is a pontifex, "a builder of a bridge between humankind and the numinous, or God."[3]

The Original Guides

Since the dawn of consciousness we human beings have been searching for "the land," the promise of fulfillment for our lives. The land represents that irresistible dream of fulfillment, or the discovery of final meaning. If only we took time to review, perhaps we would discover that certain special persons have always played a major role in guiding others through the wilderness of their meaningless lives and helping them find the bridge across the river into some partial fulfillment.

In primitive religions, each tribe had a special person who dealt with the mystery—a witch doctor, a shaman, perhaps a *chinbuki* (as in South Africa). These special persons made the wilderness bearable by explaining the shape of the terrain and the danger of the wild animals. According to the scant existing records, these persons held intercourse with the unseen world of the spirit, traveled with the dead in their flight from the body, said prayers, performed rituals, and effected cures.

As we search for the roots of spiritual guidance, our journey could take us to southern France, where prehistoric persons have left a pictorial description of daily life. There on the walls of these caves were etched people's fears, hopes, and hungers. Suppose we could see the image of a mother, a child, the hands of an old man, a bird flying through the sky. What do they all mean?

Let us imagine ourselves in a Cro-Magnon village, years before agriculture, when the way of life centered in the hunt. A mother brings her ill son to a shaman. He takes the youngster into his cave, prepares a concoction of berries and herbs, and paints the face of the child, after touching his lips with the juice. All this occurs in silence in the secret confines of the cave. In a few minutes he hands the child back to his mother, assuring her that the demon has been cast out and the boy will live.

But the fever grows hotter; the child cries through the night and on the morrow dies. Hearing the announcement, the shaman falls into a deep trance for two hours. For that period of time he is unconscious of his surroundings; he lies on the ground motionless. Then the shaman begins to stir; movement comes into his body; he arises to tell the village of his trip.

Speaking to the parents of the child but heard by all in the tribe, he tells of his flight through space as he accompanied the spirit of the boy to the world of light. He describes the smile on the departed's face when he left him to return to the village. He assures them their offspring is happy and all is well. In this way the shaman mediates between the crises of life and the divine mystery. All the mysteries of birth, drought, failed hunts, and natural calamities that befell the people were interpreted by the shaman. The community designated him to deal with the powers of the unseen world.

The mediator between life and the mystery could be a shaman like the one described or a group of elders, the old women of the tribe, or special persons chosen by some act of providence. In a magical, inexplicable way these persons negotiate with the mystery of being. Holmes calls this person a "mystagogue." "To be a mystagogue is to lead the people into the mystery that surrounds our life."[4]

Holmes makes another important point. Not only does religion demand the leadership of a special person but the community *expects* this service from one of its members. The need for a shaman, priest, or minister seems to be engraved in the human psyche. Holmes discusses three possible ways this unconscious expectation of the priest may be transmitted: genes, memes, or mind.[5] Whether this preparation for "special" religious persons comes from biological inheritance (genes), from cultural conditioning (memes), or from the collective unconscious (mind), he is not certain. Perhaps it is a combination. However it occurs, there seems to reside in the human psyche the image of a person who communicates the knowledge of the Mystery and mediates between the individual and God. Let us examine this role in the Hebraic-Christian tradition.

Guidance in Israel

While much of our knowledge of what occurred in the earliest forms of guidance may be pure speculation, we have more concrete information about the practice in ancient Israel. In Israel, Yahweh guided the people. The Law provided the form for this guidance. Priests, scribes, wise men, and prophets interpreted it and spoke for Yahweh, keeping the relation with Yahweh alive in the community. Guided by the Law, they directed the community through the wilderness (in our allegory), away from the abyss of the ocean and toward the promised land of meaning.

We must keep the Law at the center of our thinking about Israel because it gave the Israelites an orientation toward life and a way of handling the threat of meaninglessness. Israel had many types of holy men, but all were in one way or another related to the Law. According to Don Browning, the "priest, the wise man, and the scribe—each was in different ways a kind of *directeur de l'âme* [director of the soul]."[6]

Since the Law and its tradition of interpretation contained in the Torah were held in a central place in spiritual guidance for Israel, the priest had the responsibility of implementing the Law and expiating guilt when the covenant was broken. The priests gave clear expositions of the Law, and when the people realized their sinfulness, the priests mediated forgiveness through sacrifice.

Eventually these functions of expounding the Law and offering ritual sacrifices split into two roles. The priests handled the ritual, and the scribes became experts in interpreting and teaching the Law. These leaders held a prominent role in the sect of the Pharisees in Jesus' day. Unlike functionaries in many other ancient religions, their power did not depend on mystical or magical techniques but rather was oriented to the issues of everyday life.

In addition to priests and scribes were the wise men, ancient sages who knew and taught the Law. Perhaps their authority derived from tradition more than from being of a special tribe like the priests or having special call like the prophets. As bearers of the tradition they had practical wisdom in fulfilling the Law but operated independently of the priesthood.

The prophets also accepted and worked with the Law. Their particular task lay in calling Israel to accountability when the covenant was violated. The prophets paid special attention to contemporary events and Yahweh's will for the nation. These somewhat austere personalities spent little time on the guidance of individuals except in special cases like Nathan's rebuke of David and Amos's response to his accusers.

In a summary statement regarding these roles in Israel, Browning suggests that the people demanded magic and superstition of the priest and scribe. He says, "Magic is something that the masses seem to want. It promises quick solutions, wishes fulfilled, pain removed, rewards now, and this through the manipulation of both supernatural and mundane powers."[7] The spiritual guide must always be wary of the demand for magical solutions and quick cures.

wary

Jesus as Guide

The picture of Jesus formed by the preaching of the early church and recorded in the Gospels represented a different style from that of the priests and the scribes. Without a doubt Jesus knew the Law—it lay in the background of all his teaching—but he constantly reinterpreted it, searching for the spirit of the Law rather than the letter. To fulfill his mission he chose twelve followers; he invited them to be with him, to become disciples, learners. He spent time with them, showing them who he was, teaching them the meaning of his sayings, testing and preparing them to share in his mission to the world. In this intimate relation, Jesus equipped them to tell others about God's coming kingdom. Or, to place his ministry in the context of the ocean-river allegory, Jesus prepared guides to walk through the wilderness with the masses and show them the bridge that spanned the river.

Each movement in Jesus' preparation of the twelve provides a model for the task to which we have set ourselves. The call of the disciples provides the foundation for the task of guidance. Command and promise came together: "Follow me and I will make you become fishers of men" (Mark 1:17). The guide must first become a follower.

The follower learns through observation. Jesus showed them the meaning of the kingdom in exorcising the demon (Mark 1:21–28), healing Simon's mother-in-law (1:29–31), rising early for prayer (1:35–39), and cleansing the leper (1:40–45). The best way to train persons in the ministry of the kingdom is to show them through example.

After demonstrating the kingdom to a number of disciples, he chose twelve, that they should "be with him" (Mark 3:14). Jesus formed these diverse followers of his into a tightly knit community. The spiritual life does not grow in isolation from others but through sharing and living together.

To those who were chosen to "be with him," he taught the principles of the kingdom (see Mark 4:1–32). Instruction only makes sense to persons who have chosen to live a kingdom life, and instruction is given in community to shape a corporate mentality and build mutual support. Serious guides need the support of a community.

With the proper preparation Jesus called the twelve to himself and sent them out to participate in the work (Mark 6:7–13). The calling, the demonstration, the community building, and the instruction combined to prepare guides to participate in the mission of Christ. They were not mature, they had no natural power, nor did they have education or wealth. What they had was an intimate knowledge of Christ, and he sent them to share with others what they had learned.

Obviously, the mission of the twelve was successful. The number of workers multiplied, and later Jesus was able to send out seventy (Luke 10:1–20). Perhaps the apostles used the same method Jesus had used with them. The spiritual guides multiplied and were sent forth. At their return we see one other element in the method of Jesus. They rejoiced that the devils were subject to them and Jesus corrected them: "Do not rejoice in this, that the spirits are subject to you; but rejoice that your names are written in heaven" (Luke 10:20). Jesus as the master guide corrected their focus and priorities.

This model suggests to us the movements in Jesus' method of preparation. His way still has practical relevance for our calling and equipping spiritual guides.

After Jesus had prepared and sent out the twelve, he seemed to use public preaching to the multitudes and private conversations with individuals as his means of helping persons connect with God (see, for example, Matt. 5–7, public preaching; Matt. 8:1–4, private conversation). Jesus always intended to relate persons consciously with God.

This example of Jesus provided the standard for his followers: they witnessed publicly to the masses and spoke face-to-face with individuals. Peter, for example, proclaimed the gospel to a crowd of several thousand on the day of Pentecost (Acts 2:14–36). But he also went to Simon the tanner's house to rest and doubtless to strengthen Simon's faith (Acts 9:36–43). He then accepted an invitation from Cornelius, to talk with him and with family members and servants about Christ (Acts 10). In this encounter, the Spirit of Christ came upon Cornelius and his household. God had already spoken to Cornelius, but the witness and explanation of a believer like Peter refined and focused his faith and introduced him to Jesus Christ.

Another instance of guidance centered in a layman's encounter with Saul of Tarsus (Acts 9:1–19). Saul, an angry Jew, had orders to destroy the Christians at Damascus. But as he journeyed to Damascus, he met the risen Christ (9:5). This encounter came about because of the faithful witness of Stephen, a believer who had spoken to

Saul before he left on the trip (Acts 7:54–60), and because of the risky obedience of another disciple, Ananias, after he arrived in Damascus (9:10–19). Stephen's witness to Christ and his courage in death was certainly used by Christ to awaken Saul, but the conversion was not complete until Ananias, a lay believer in Damascus, followed the guidance of the Lord and came to Saul, laid his hands upon him, and baptized him. The introduction of persons to the faith always involves public and private guidance.

This person-to-person expansion of the faith provided the chief approach of the early church. Two of the great church historians underscore this fact. Adolph Harnack says, "It is impossible to see in any one class of people inside the church the chief agents of the Christian propaganda." On the other hand "we cannot hesitate to believe that the great mission of Christianity was in reality accomplished by means of informal missionaries."[8]

To this penetrating analysis Kenneth S. Latourette adds that "the chief agents in the expansion of Christianity appear not to have been those who made it a profession or made it a major part of their occupation, but men and women who carried on their livelihood in some purely secular manner and spoke of their faith to those they met in this natural fashion."[9]

No better example of lay evangelism can be found than Philip's encounter with the eunuch of Queen Candace's court. While Philip was in Samaria, the messenger of the Lord instructed him to go to Gaza. There he encountered the eunuch, riding in a chariot and reading Isaiah:

> As a sheep led to the slaughter
> Or a lamb before its shearer is dumb,
> so he opens not his mouth.
> In his humiliation justice was denied him.
> Who can describe his generation?
> For his life is taken up from the earth.
>
> Acts 8:32–33

Philip asked the eunuch, "Do you understand what you're reading?"

To this inquiry, the eunuch said, "How can I, unless someone guides me?" Philip began with that concern and told him the good news about Jesus. One person guided another person in the knowledge of the faith.

Desert Fathers and Mothers as Guides

The spontaneous sharing of the faith accounted for the rapid expansion of believers during the first three centuries, until Constantine made the new faith lawful in the Roman Empire. Whether this official recognition served the purpose of God or only served to dilute the faith will continue to be debated throughout the life of the church. No matter how we decide this issue, the answer seemed obvious to a number of devout souls of the fourth century. They interpreted this decision of Constantine as apostasy and fled to the Egyptian desert to seek their own salvation.

During the Roman persecutions one of the highest forms of devotion to Christ had been martyrdom. Following the Edict of Milan in 313 A.D., which stopped the persecution of Christians, deeply pious souls sought their martyrdom in the sands of the desert. In a story about one of these recluses, Henri Nouwen makes clear what this retreat to the desert meant.

Abba (father) Arsenius, an educated Roman who served in the court of Emperor Theodosius, prayed for the Lord to lead him in the way of salvation.

In response to his prayer, a voice said to him, "Arsenius, flee from the world and you will be saved." Being obedient, Arsenius made his way to Alexandria and into the desert.

In the desert he prayed again for the Lord to lead him in the way of salvation. Again, the voice: "Arsenius, flee, be silent, pray always, for these are the sources of sinlessness." According to Nouwen, "The words flee, be silent, and pray summarize the spirituality of the desert."[10]

Perhaps as many as 20,000 souls took up residence in caves and desert communities to find their own salvation in the manner of Arsenius. They remained in the desert, some for fifteen or twenty years, without ever speaking to a soul. Because of the insights they gained and the spiritual power they possessed, many persons came to them for counsel, for healing, and for spiritual guidance. Stories of miracles, spiritual insights, and healings fill the literature of these desert saints.

In the silence of the desert, they achieved a wisdom that nourished many empty souls in the newly established church of Constantine. It is reported that even Constantine himself went to Egypt to seek guidance from Anthony (c. 250–350). These wisdom figures, for the most part, were lay persons—men and women.

With respect to guidance, there must be a connection between the rugged discipline of solitude, silence, and prayer and the spiritual energy that empowered these men and women to be directors of souls. Guidance of others always requires appropriate preparation. Is it not interesting that those who fled to the deserts were soon sought as spiritual guides?

After a couple of hundred years, the model of the desert saint, both the hermitic and the communal type, gave way to the monastic movements of the fifth and sixth centuries. The great monastic leaders, from Benedict of Nursia onward, commended spiritual direction to the members of the community. In the pre-Reformation church, leaders like Columba (c. 527–597), Gregory the Great (c. 540–604), and Aethelred (c. 968–1016) emphasized the importance of a soul friend to offer guidance on the spiritual journey.

The Reformation

Various forms of spiritual guidance emerged in the Reformation. In the Reformed church, John Calvin (1509–1564) gave major attention to preaching. Hearing the word of God proclaimed and taught was a new experience for the people. These twin emphases provided corporate spiritual guidance for believers during the Reformation period.

The most outstanding contribution of the Reformation in expanding spiritual awakening was placing the scriptures in the hands of the laity. Heretofore dependent on priests for hearing and interpreting the Bible, the laity could now read and apply the word of God to their own lives. The availability of the written word proved to be a spiritually formative influence.

In addition to preaching, the leaders of the new church emphasized creeds and confessions as forms of spiritual guidance. Confessions summarized biblical truth in a form that spoke to current issues in the church's life. The people read, studied, memorized, and reflected on these scriptural summaries of the faith. Such condensations of the teachings of scripture strengthened and formed the lives of liberated believers.

The Reformers gave great care to writing and teaching catechisms—instructional manuals of basic questions and answers about the substance of the Christian faith. The catechisms drew heavily on the ten commandments, the creeds of the church, and the Lord's Prayer—the foundational statements of the Christian faith. These manuals gave spiritual guidance to the children of the Reformation.

In addition to preaching and providing the scriptures, confessions, and catechisms to laity, men like Luther and Calvin also gave personal guidance to individuals. The *Table Talk* of Martin Luther (1483–1546) and the massive correspondence of Calvin give evidence of their abilities as spiritual guides. Though this guidance may not have been offered in a formal relationship, it functioned to support and direct persons on their spiritual journeys.

Spiritual guidance in the Reformation focused on the word of God—hearing, reading, and doing. Most of the guidance was corporate and instructional in nature, methods appropriate for the context.

The influence of this model of spiritual guidance can be discerned a century later in England in the ministry of Richard Baxter (1615–1691). In the midst of a busy schedule, Baxter and his assistant set aside two days each week to instruct persons in the faith. He aimed to visit with seven families each day, fourteen each week. The conversation focused on the catechism: he asked the family to recite the catechism, he explained the meaning to them, he modestly inquired into the state of their souls, and then sought to send them home with the resolve to live for God. Baxter evaluated his ministry thus: "Of all the works that ever I attempted this yielded me most comfort in the practice of it."[11]

In the eighteenth century another form of direction emerged which must also trace its roots to the Reformation—the Wesleyan revival. After an experience at Aldersgate in 1738 when his heart was "strangely warmed," John Wesley (1703–1791) began preaching to the miners and other working classes. When the churches refused to embrace his ministry, Wesley preached in the open air. His proclamation of the gospel produced powerful emotions and dramatic responses in his hearers. Thousands were converted to Christ.

While this style opened many to faith and started them on their Christian journey, it would be fair to say that the results of Wesley and his followers were preserved by the establishment of a unique kind of group. Following a conversion experience, new converts were formed into cells called "class meetings," whose members met once each week and reported on the state of their souls. Questions like diligence in prayer, confession of sin, contributions to the ministry, and service to those in need were covered. When anyone became slack in performance or began to miss meetings, class leaders called on them and helped restore them to the faith.

The proclamation of the gospel to the masses and the cultivation of decisions in class meetings provide another model of spiritual guidance. Wesley combined the emphasis on proclamation we find in Calvin with the pastoral care found in Baxter and in so doing offered an effective model of spiritual guidance.

What has the modern church done with these powerful models of ministering to the needs of individuals? As we have hinted, a subtle but definitive transition occurred between the eighteenth and twentieth centuries, a transition that shifted the focus from salvation to self-realization. Brooks Holifield has succinctly summarized that change: "The story [of pastoral care] proceeds from an ideal of self-denial to one of self-love, from self-love to self-culture, from self-culture to self-mastery, from self-mastery to self-realization within a trustworthy culture, and finally to a later form of self-realization counterposed against cultural mores and social institutions."[12]

In the latter years of the twentieth century, church leaders whose roots spring from the Reformation sought to give a renewed emphasis to spiritual direction in the church.[13] In many ways, the pastoral care movement replaced the role of the spiritual guide. For a period, it seemed little more than a secular psychology embraced by the church, but this is now being corrected. Competent leaders in the movement have begun to reclaim the theological and ethical depths of pastoral care.[14]

Images of Spiritual Direction

Perhaps some insight into the task of evangelism as spiritual guidance can be gained from an examination of the various names given to the spiritual guide. A contemporary designation of the spiritual director is that of "spiritual friend." A spiritual friend is a person who can be present in the crises of life when one's vision and outlook have been threatened. Tilden Edwards describes a woman who had been a social activist, sought therapy, had a good family life, but in a crisis of soul had no one to whom she could entrust her deepest sense of need.[15] She needed a spiritual friend.

A spiritual friend stands with another in his or her time of trouble and offers support and guidance in the awareness of God. This person recognizes those in crisis and moves into the fray with them. True friendship takes initiative and, in love, engages the pain and struggle of another.

Another designation, "faithful friend," has been emphasized by Dorothy Deavers, who acknowledges that this term is borrowed from Frances de Sales.[16] Such a guide must be faithful, both to God, to the other, and to himself or herself.

In the Russian Orthodox Church, these guides were known as "old men," *staretz.* A *staretz* always had age, which indicated maturity and spiritual wisdom. Our spiritual guide need not be old, or male, but should at least have wisdom in the ways of God with the soul.

Morton Kelsey has called the spiritual director "a companion on the inner way."[17] Nearly half a century ago, C. G. Jung stated that the first half of life was spent building the persona, an appearance to the world, and the second half in discovering the inner world of the soul. Building on this notion, Kelsey suggests that persons need companions on this inward search. If the journey requires companionship, certainly the beginning of the journey requires no less. The person who introduces another to the faith journey will certainly deal with the life story, the previous struggles, and other blocks that may inhibit faith. Thus the definition of companion who goes inward with another rightly describes one of the roles of the evangelist.

Some Implications for Evangelism

From the dawn of human consciousness persons have sought spiritual guidance. Be they superstitious natives or Israelites in the wilderness or men and women of today, human beings need help in answering the deep questions of human existence.

To meet this need we have discovered in our brief historical review that there has always been a person or group of persons to help questioners deal with the Mystery. These designated guides focused on questions about the origin of life, the calamities that befall human beings, and death.

The method of the guide has changed through time. Differences in the perception of persons and alternating visions of the Mystery gave rise to different styles. When the unconscious was described by Freud, spiritual guides had to take account of deeper drives and motivations. With the Reformation emphasis on grace, spiritual direction was driven to acknowledge that human merit or works do not earn God's favor.

We must also acknowledge that the role of the guide has been vulnerable to excesses and abuse. Guides may become too authoritarian or too lax; guides may substitute their will for the will of God. So a guide must be sensitive to perversions and subject to accountability.

At many stages in life, persons need an authority, a mentor, or a director for their lives. Evidence shows that adolescence is one such time when a mentor is needed, someone to emulate. But other crises require strength and reassurance too. An adult in search of a vital faith needs information and support. Questions and issues arise in the lives of all believers, and they need someone to give them guidance.

3

The Theological Structure of Spiritual Guidance

From the beginning there have been those who "spoke for God and spoke about God" to other persons. To further assist in making this task approachable, we must now define a faith structure within which initial spiritual guidance functions.

"What has theology to do with the 'real' experience of Christ?" I have been asked that question dozens of times by sincere lay men and women. And laity are not alone; many ordained ministers bypass the rigors of clear, systematic thought and focus on practical techniques.

Both these responses have validity. Surely the firsthand experience of Christ differs from the rational formulation of Christian experience in the creeds. Perhaps the contrast is as great as the person who looks at the Atlantic Ocean and then goes off and consults a map.

When you look at a map of the ocean, you see no boisterous waves, no white fluffy clouds, nor do you feel the breeze off the water. But when you hold a map in your hands, you have a compilation of others' experiences collected over the years. If you were only taking a walk on the beach or going for an afternoon cruise, no map would be necessary; but if you intend to sail the ocean, the map is essential. Without it you would soon be lost, and the consequences of sailing blind would be disastrous.[1]

Like a map, theology gives us the composite thinking of

many persons who have experienced Christ, and thus it offers much more to the spiritual guide than a single personal experience. It is important to spell out a larger frame of reference, the faith structure, that informs spiritual guidance.

For our purposes, the faith structure of the spiritual guide must include both a corporate and a personal dimension—what we believe about God, the world, and the church and, in a limited, more personal sense, what we believe about the relation of God to the subject and the guide. The larger frame of reference of God/world/church defines the arena in which the social, corporate witness must be made. The God/guide/subject relationship functions within the larger, more inclusive context. A consideration of the interrelation of the two dimensions of faith saves the guide from a privatism that separates personal experience from social responsibility. Picture the relationship of the corporate and personal faith structures as two overlapping triangles: God/world/church and God/guide/subject; the first shapes the mission of the church, the latter informs the tasks of spiritual guidance.

The God/World/Church Triad

The tasks of spiritual guidance occur within the larger triad of God/world/church (see Figure 3). What we believe about God stands at the center of this relation—who God is, how God relates to the world, how God relates to the church. In our perspective, God is the source of the world; the creation occurs through the intention of God. Perhaps love and will are the most basic affirmations that can be made of Yahweh—that God loves and purposes. Can we not say that the loving intention of the divine presence stands behind all that is and all that occurs? Will precedes all being! Without the divine intention, nothing would be. This divine intention manifests itself in the energy of love, a force that effects change.

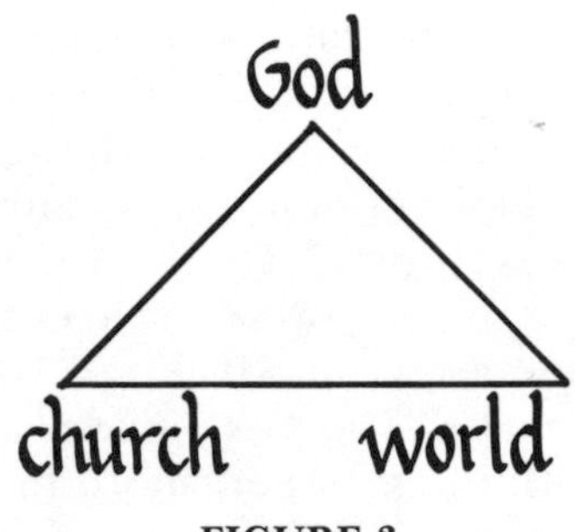

FIGURE 3.

God

According to the biblical record, the divine will that precedes all things expressed itself first in creation. "In the beginning God . . . " And God said, "Let there be . . . " (Gen. 1, 3, 6, 14). This divine intention expressed itself in a word, a creative word that called the world into being. "By faith we understand that the world was created by the word of God" (Heb. 11:3). In every moment of the world's existence, this speech of God creates and sustains it.

God not only purposed and created but reconciled those who failed to fulfill the divine purpose. When God's original intention did not reach fulfillment, God reached out to the fallen and reestablished the eternal purpose. Remember the Lord's question to Adam in the garden, "Where are you?" (Gen. 3:9). Or recollect the call to Abram to begin a long process of revelation in the nation Israel (Gen. 12:1–3).

The creation and reconciliation indicate that God intended to realize a purpose in this world, in its history. The created world is the theater in which the will of God is to be realized. If the world forms the theater of God's action, what is it like?

The World

The world, the material creation, though created by God and given order through natural laws, has not always functioned as God intended. Aberrations in nature—storms, earthquakes, deformed births—are signs of imperfection, if not rebellion; these aspects of nature at least indicate its incompleteness.

Even the structures of social life, the greed of corporations, and the ambitions of governments illustrate the misdirections of life on the planet. Certainly God did not intend human life to be plagued with alienation, oppression, and war, but such has marked the history of human striving. Yet this world is the one which God made and reconciled and the one in which the divine purpose will be realized. But how?

The Church

This question calls for the third corner of the triad—the church. The church, as the body of Christ, has the mission to re-present Jesus Christ; it is a corporate expression of his person. As a religious entity among other social, political, and business aspects of the culture, the church has as its mission the transformation of the culture with the Spirit of Christ—love, justice, compassion, purpose.

As a community of Christ, the church works toward a reconciled society in which alienation is overcome and loving relations are created between persons and groups. The church seeks justice for the oppressed—freedom, equality, and the satisfaction of needs. Within history, the church bears witness to God's presence and purposes, endeavoring to infuse history with meaning.

In a discussion of spiritual guidance you could reasonably ask, Why have we introduced this larger triad of God, world, and church? Does not this corporate discussion seem far away from the intimate encounter of one person with another? This structure defines the largest horizon in which the person-to-person relation occurs; it conditions and defines this one-to-one encounter. To assume that ministry in this larger theater meets the demands of personal faith and discipleship would be as great an error as to have no vision beyond individual conversion. The church of Jesus Christ, to be effective in history, seeks the transformation of individuals so that they may become transformers of history. The structures of the church and of society also have an influence on the transformation of individuals; the personal and social are mutually interactive and cannot be separated.

Theologically, the larger structure defines the context within which spiritual guidance occurs. God cares about the world—its groups, societies, and nations—but God loves the individuals who compose the societies and the nations. God has commissioned the church to bear witness to the world, a task achieved through the church's mission. And God calls persons to share their faith with individuals, a goal achieved through personal witness.

God, Guides, and Subjects

Within the God/world/church structure, a smaller relational structure also exists: the God/guide/subject triad (see Figure 4). Although the latter derives from the larger faith structure, it provides an essential form for the transformative role of spiritual guidance. What we believe about God, guides, and persons defines the faith structure within which spiritual guidance is offered. Because of the sensitive nature of the task of one person guiding another into faith, it is necessary to define the faith structure in which it occurs.

In this faith structure our understanding of God remains constant with that in the larger triad, but it requires a slightly different focus. God created persons in

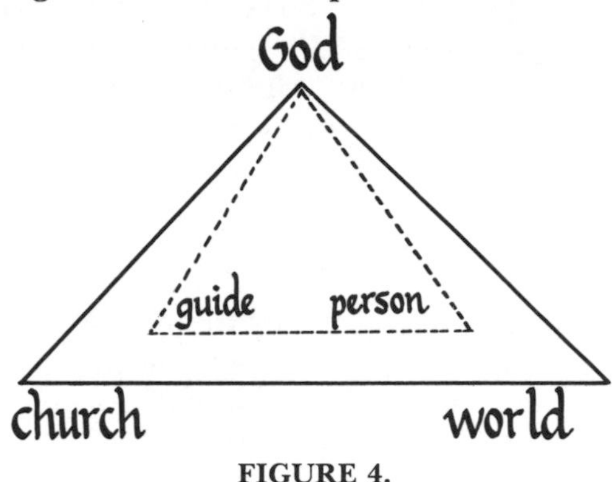

FIGURE 4.

the divine image; they share a kinship with and hunger for the divine (Gen. 1:26–27). In Jesus Christ, God has already reconciled all persons to godself, a historical act (2 Cor. 5:17–21). God has poured forth the Holy Spirit upon the cosmos, upon all flesh, seeking to awaken all humanity to the redemption in Jesus Christ (John 16:8–11, Acts 2:17). Salvation or participation in the reconciliation with God in Christ begins when one trusts in Christ by grace, a gift of God (Eph. 2:8–9). Through obedience, those who are reconciled begin to fulfill the intention of God in their personal lives.

Just as the church has a corporate mission to society in re-presenting Jesus Christ to the world, those who are members of the church also have the task of discerning the presence of Christ in individuals, bearing witness to the good news of God's love, and modeling in their lifestyle the Spirit of Christ.

The ministry of one person to another has its grounding in the church's larger mission—to re-present Christ to the world. Every member of Christ's body has a share in this mandate (1 Cor. 12:27). The authority for this total participation in the mission derives from the priesthood of all believers (1 Peter 2:9–10). To be a believer in Christ, to be baptized into his body, connects each one to Christ and mediates to the baptized an authority for ministry. This responsibility for ministry and the authority to fulfill this calling permeates the Christian vocation in the world. We are exploring one aspect of this call, the introduction of persons to a vital, personal faith that is foundational for all ministry.

The Guide

We can identify four aspects of the ministry of one person to another: discernment, witness, host, and model.

The priest, the believer ordained by baptism, must be a discerner of Christ's presence in another. **Discernment** depends upon receiving data from the subject in the narrative of his or her life. The tools for receiving these data are a few, simple, basic questions and a listening ear. When the spiritual guide gathers these data, she or he can then begin to identify the presence and activity of Christ in a person's life. This pre-evangelism marks the beginning point of spiritual guidance. Thus guidance begins not with our experience, or our faith, or even Christ's mandates, but with the presence and activity of Christ in the life of the subject. The narrative of the subject provides both the context and the agenda of the guide.[2]

While the task begins with listening and discernment, it does not remain passive but includes active **witness**. Though not inevitable, listening to another usually provokes that person to ask the guide about his or her faith. Faith shared in response to a query creates less disturbance than a witness dropped like a rock in a pond. The guide may respond in two ways: a personal vignette or a statement of the gospel.

The personal vignette narrates a portion of the guide's own faith story. To be effective this short narrative should respond to the subject's narrative, it should state clearly the guide's own experience of Christ, and it should be brief. The guide should not intimidate the subject with experiences beyond that person's grasp, should not answer questions the subject is not asking, should not endeavor to manipulate the subject's feelings. And, perhaps most important of all, guides should not make themselves the center of attention.

Perhaps the best image of this relationship between spiritual guide and subject is that of a bridge. The spiritual guide offers the subject a connecting point with the body of Christ; the connection becomes a bridge over which the subject may walk into a relationship with the guide and the guide's community. Recall how Urban Holmes described the "pontifex": a builder of bridges. If at first the bridge looks too treacherous, too narrow, or too difficult, the subject will have difficulty taking the first step into the community. Seasoned guides build safe bridges.

In addition to sharing a faith experience, the guide also gives witness to biblical truth—the gospel. The essential gospel includes a witness to the human condition, the grace of God, and an invitation to respond in faith. An informed and properly prepared guide should know a dozen or so scriptures that declare these basic truths of the gospel. If these verses are not committed to memory, the guide should know, at least, the substance of the text.

The guide serves not only as a discerner and witness but also as a gracious **host**. Consider the roles of a host: a host issues personal invitations to guests, receives them when they arrive, directs them to the refreshments, and introduces them to others. This hospitable image of the spiritual guide provides the agenda for initiating new persons into the worshiping community. Upon their response to Christ, the host becomes an official welcomer in behalf of Christ. Guides also describe to new family members the importance of worship, service, and the study of scripture. When the guide introduces a new believer to other persons, these fellow believers begin to share the task of support and guidance, thus relieving the initial guide of the total responsibility for nurture and growth.

Obviously, one guide cannot have the best discernment or the most effective witness for everyone. Indeed, a guide need not, because the entire priesthood of the believing community offers an assortment of gifts and possibilities to the person seeking faith. Whether or not each member of the Christian fellowship embraces the role of spiritual guide, this believing community forms the context for the discovery and nurture of faith.

In this triadic relation of God/guide/subject, the spiritual guide fills yet another important role—as a living **model**. Some aspects of the Christian life cannot be reduced to words and descriptions; they must be demonstrated. Most persons receive their greatest impetus for being a follower of Christ from the example set by others. Thus the spiritual guide models the Christian life for subjects and shows them what it means to be on a faith journey. A newly believing person learns the basics of the Christian life by imitation; one person copies another, as in the early church, where Paul said to the Corinthians, "I urge you, then, be imitators of me" (1 Cor. 4:16).

The lifestyle of the guide must fuse concern for persons and concern for the larger society. In this living model, the subject encounters, at the beginning of the Christian journey, a conviction that the knowledge of Christ demands a radical involvement in the issues confronting the human race. When modeled by the guide, this responsibility does not come as a new law, or a requirement for salvation, but rather as a practical demonstration of how the Christian lives.

The Subject of Guidance

Thus far in our examination of the two triadic structures with the purposive God at the apex, we have examined the will of God for the church in its relation to the world, and we have set forth the role of members of the body of Christ as guiding persons into the faith. This structure also demands an exploration of the subject. How we define the subject determines both why and how we make our approach.

In our faith perspective, the subject has been created in the image of God (Gen. 1:27). While always a contingent being, however, the person can say, "I am": that is, "I am and I am conscious that I am." In the power of this self-awareness, persons ask the meaning of their lives, a query that includes one's origin, identity, purpose, and destiny.[3] Although these questions are asked with existential seriousness, persons cannot find their meaning within themselves; meaning must come to them as a gift in a personal disclosure. This bondage and the consequent helplessness result from sin. Human beings are estranged from what God intended and created them to be.

Persons experience this estranged condition as a restlessness, anxiety, a persistent drive, an unsatisfied hunger for meaning. In efforts to calm their restlessness, persons focus on one goal after another; they give their loyalty to a lover, a spouse, family, success, and symbols of security like wealth, insurance, or the production of arms. One by one, time and circumstance erode human confidence in these false securities.

Another characteristic of the subject is that she or he creates and carries the meaning of life in a narrative, a personal story of her or his search. This capacity for narrative makes human beings historical creatures; they experience events in time and interpret those events, combining their meaning with their remembered past and their anticipated future. In the act of interpreting and relating, human beings create continuity expressed in their life story.

This life story not only creates continuity, it carries personal identity. A person *is* the story that she or he tells. From one perspective, a person may be more than the story told, but always the story defines self-identity. To know persons, therefore, one must know their story. When we share the gospel with others, it always produces a change in their perception of themselves. Conversion in a personal life means the alteration of their story. If the story carries both their meaning and their identity, change requires an enormous risk, and their resistance is overcome only by the promise of wholeness and release from the pain of meaninglessness.

Pain does not always precipitate change; sometimes the fear of change is greater than the pain. Numerous fears beset the searching soul. People frequently have a fear of God, generated by childhood images. For them, God has been depicted as a heinous power that punishes children who break parental rules.

This negative image of God may also arise out of children's relationship with their parents. Since the images we use to symbolize God derive from our relationship with our dominant parent, a negative parental relationship provides a fearful image of God.[4]

For others, the fear may be not of the image of God but of a loss of autonomy. In a culture characterized by individualism—"to be human is to be free to choose what one wills"—to surrender to God seems to imply the sacrifice of personal freedom. So some modern persons resist commitment to Christ because it appears to sacrifice their freedom and personhood.

Still others resist alteration of their lives because they fear the unknown. They reason that at least in their present condition they know the risks of life. Even if unfulfilled, their present lifestyle has a familiarity that poses as security.

For other persons, the risk may be not the unknown but the known. They have a clear idea that a response to God entails a radical shift in lifestyle, such as the breaking off of a clandestine relationship or confessing a personal wrong. These demands evoke fear too great to handle, and resistance grows until the pain within outweighs the threat without.

Resistance sometimes comes because of a negative perception of Christian commitment, such as the fear of religious fanaticism. Perhaps these persons have seen radical conversions in their families, or have been accosted by offensive witnesses, or have felt threatened by their own shadow side. Whatever the source of fear, these persons must be convinced that God does not make religious fanatics.

The Subject and the Spiritual Guide

To this point, we have described the subject from a human perspective: a self-conscious, seeking, narrating creature who often resists change. This perspective can be verified by listening to the subject's stories. But the spiritual guide has a second vision—depth perception, if you will. This alternative perspective presupposes the active presence of God in another's life. God's gracious, inclusive love reaches out to all persons from the beginning of their lives, perhaps from eternity.

The spiritual guide presupposes that God has been at work in the life of the subject since the day of birth. God created this person, loved this person, reconciled him or her in Jesus Christ. God has given the Spirit to all persons, drawing each one to Christ. This faith gives the spiritual guide a particular posture toward the subject; it also provides a filter to hear the life story.

Subjects may or may not have consciously identified the presence of the Spirit in their lives. The Spirit, in a variety of ways, has acted upon the subject, but until that person has a conscious encounter with Christ, the activity of the Spirit remains unconscious.

How can the spiritual guide uncover the work of the Spirit and make the subject conscious of Christ? The ability to perceive Christ requires a vital faith. The better the guides know Christ, the more sensitive they will be to the presence of Christ in others. This discernment is less a logical deduction and more a contemplative imagining, an active visioning of Christ in the subject.

But how do we perceive? We examine the narrative through gospel lenses or filters. The narrative reveals the hunger and striving for meaning; it expresses the brokenness and emptiness of a life; it points out the highest moments of fulfillment. The trained, sensitive ear of the spiritual guide, conditioned by the gospel, discerns the Spirit and seeks to make the subject aware of the depth dimension of his or her own narrative.

A Case History

Several months ago I came to my office and looked at the calendar to find out what lay before me for the day. My eyes fell on the name Will Stone.

"Who is Will Stone?" I asked my secretary.

She did not know. He had called to make an appointment to talk with me but gave no other details about himself. About that time, Will arrived in my office.

"I'm from the Peachtree Hills Presbyterian Church," he began, "and my pastor, James R. Smith—a friend of yours, I believe—has left and I have no one to talk with. Jimmy was about my age and seemed to understand me when I had a problem, but now he is gone. Since I heard you speak at our church, I thought you might be able to help me."

I told him I would be glad to try.

"I graduated from Georgia Tech in engineering," he began, "and I have never been able to get faith to fit. I have a mathematical, analytical mentality, and faith always felt like believing something that you knew wasn't true."

"Tell me about your church experience," I suggested.

"I was reared in the church. My parents took me to church since before I can remember. They're on the search committee to find a new preacher since Jim left. I've had quite a bit of church."

"But you're having problems with your beliefs?"

"Yes. I guess my wife triggered it. She's been taking courses in religion at Mercer [a church-related college], and she's been getting deeper and deeper into religion. I don't want my doubts to discourage her."

"I appreciate your sensitivity."

"But," he continued, "I just don't know how to believe."

"What is your idea of God? What sort of picture do you hold of God?" I asked.

In response to this question he talked about twenty

minutes. He didn't respond to my question but rehearsed why he couldn't believe in God and how he had a scientific, technological mentality.

"Has there ever been a time in your life when God did seem real to you?" I asked, trying to refocus the conversation.

He replied immediately. "Yes. When I was a Boy Scout I rescued a fellow who was drowning." He had a feeling of pride in having saved someone. "Then I remember putting out a fire in a neighbor's apartment. She was an elderly widow who had forgotten to turn off her stove. When I doused the flames and helped her get out, I felt I had done something worthwhile."

He spoke another ten or fifteen minutes about this experience and how good it made him feel to do something for someone else. The conversation seemed bogged down and our time together was running out.

"Will, you seem to be looking for this God in whom you have difficulty believing—you care about your wife, you made an appointment to come talk, you have shared several important experiences of faith—and it appears to me that you may be searching for something you have been unable to name."

Will reflected silently on what I had said.

"But, Will, you've spent forty minutes telling me why you don't believe. Much of what you say sounds like rationalizations. I wonder if you really believe them yourself."

I knew a bold statement was risky, but how was I to help Will if he continued to strengthen his walls of defense? Then I looked into Will's eyes and saw sheer terror. His neat defense had shattered and he stood emotionally naked, for the moment anyway.

"Will, those rationalizations protect you from God and from yourself. It's scary as hell to face yourself in the presence of God."

We sat together in silence for a few moments.

"I wonder if you would be willing to use another side of your mind. In your technical training you have developed an active, rational mode of consciousness in which you seek data, form hypotheses, test them, and evaluate your discoveries. I wonder if you'd be willing to engage in an experiment with another approach to reality."

"What's that?" he asked.

"I want to invite you to adopt a receptive mode of consciousness, to be present to truth or ideas without feeling you must analyze them—simply be open and receptive to them. I urge you to think of yourself as a 'seeker' for truth rather than a skeptic."

After waiting a moment for the challenge to sink in, I made a suggestion. "Read the Gospel of Mark. Adopt the posture that God can be seen in Jesus. See if God will not communicate godself to you through the biblical record. Read the text with openness, receptivity."

I gave Will a book I thought would be helpful to him, offered him a few suggestions, and promised to write.

In the weeks that passed I thought a number of times about my encounter with Will. He lived in an Enlightenment world of reason, which constructed reality from what he had experienced with his five senses. I believe in Will's world, but I also believe in the worlds I have described in those two triadic structures. Behind and within the visible world there exists a power that created and sustains it. I believe this creative power is personal and seeks to become known in the consciousness of human beings.

As is so often the case in spiritual guidance, Will and I experienced a collision of worlds—the rational world open to sensory perception and the spiritual world accessible only to faith. To be an effective guide, one must understand the subject's vision of the world and how God relates to it as well as the world in which the subject lives.

What aspects of this interview seem to be germane to Will's coming into a vital faith experience? What is his faith perspective and how does my perspective interface with it?

First, it is worth noting that this interview was initiated by Will and came out of the blue. It took a lot of courage for him to make an appointment with someone who did not know him.

He introduced his problem as one of "faith." When he described his view of reality as conditioned by a technological mind-set, he told me that his view lacked a God dimension. At this point I realized that my vision of the triadic structures and his flat perspective of reality would collide. How could I help him consider an alternative vision?

His church experience had provided very little for him to build on. Most of his remembered experiences were superficial. His memories of God did not arise from the church, or from a deep sense of being known by God, but from his rescuing others. First he saved a boy from drowning, then a woman from being burned in her apartment. These experiences point to a God who is pleased with us when we do good.

Will's issue had become acute through his wife's pursuit of religion. Her deepened interest sharpened his awareness of his doubts. He did not wish his unbelief to dampen her faith.

A number of things about Will commend him. He took the initiative to seek me out; he acknowledged his problem and the source of it; he had compassion for his wife and desired to protect her growing faith. All these aspects of his character indicate the work of the Spirit of God in Will's life, evidences of the Spirit seeking his reconciliation.

I cannot make Will see God by telling him my insight into his experience. He will not understand my words. My task is, I believe, to invite Will to change his analytical approach to a receptive one. I asked him to open himself to the God who speaks through Christ in the narratives of the Bible.

In this encounter, I hoped to be a helpful spiritual guide by taking Will's life story seriously, seeking to discern the divine presence in his life, and bearing witness to him in a way that he could receive it. I was aware that this personal engagement occurred in the larger triad of God/world/church and must never become isolated as a private experience of God.

From Will's story it appears that the church had sought to carry out its mission without effectively incorporating him into its life. The larger triad of God/world/church provides the theater within which the task of spiritual guidance occurs, and the guidance of persons into a conscious experience of faith provides the dynamic energy for the body of Christ.

4

The Style of the Spiritual Guide

Having defined personal evangelism as spiritual guidance, and having discussed the role of the spiritual guide in the history of faith and the twin triads within which guidance occurs, we must now look more deeply at the manner in which the Spirit of Christ comes to a person.

Is it not startling that the one style of communicating the faith to persons that has been embraced by thousands has been utterly rejected by a like number? I refer to the "Evangelism Explosion" model of D. James Kennedy and others like it. This model offers a simple, direct approach to presenting the essence of the gospel to an individual in ten or fifteen minutes or less.

A number of very positive things can be said for this model: it is biblical, simple, reproducible, workable, lay-oriented, and demonstrably effective. But scores of leaders in mainline churches have rejected the approach as inappropriate, simplistic, abrupt, manipulative, and unfaithful to the whole gospel. Before exploring their reasons for this judgment, we should more fully describe the model that produces such diverse evaluations.

When James Kennedy graduated from Columbia Theological Seminary, he was called to a new church development in Fort Lauderdale, Florida. He began with forty-five persons, and in the course of a year the number dwindled to a mere seventeen. At this point of crisis he was invited to conduct a series of evangelistic services for a church in Decatur, Georgia. The experience of that week proved to be a turning point in his ministry.

The host minister of the Decatur church indicted that Kennedy would be preaching each evening, but during the day the two of them would be visiting persons in their homes to present the gospel of Christ. During that week the old minister showed Kennedy how to proclaim the gospel to persons in a face-to-face setting and to lead them to a personal faith in Christ. After seeing fifty-four persons come to Christ through their combined efforts, Kennedy says, "I went back to Fort Lauderdale a new man, and I began to do just what I had seen done."[1]

Following this life-changing experience, Kennedy systematized what he had learned and organized it into a teachable, reproducible format. His outline for the presentation of the gospel is in three parts—Introduction, Presentation, Conclusion—much like a sermon. Although this approach to sharing the faith does not differ greatly from that taught by Campus Crusade for Christ ("The Four Spiritual Laws") or the "Roman Road to Salvation" (used frequently by Southern Baptists), we will examine Evangelism Explosion as representative of this particular confrontational model.

In the introductory phase of the presentation, the witness seeks to discover pertinent information about the subject's life and church background. When this contact has been firmly established, the witness tells about the church she or he attends and then gives a personal testimony of faith in Christ. The testimony sets the stage to ask the subject two important questions:

1. "Have you come to a place in your spiritual life where you know for certain that if you were to die today you would go to heaven?"

2. "Suppose that you were to die tonight and stand before God and He were to say to you, 'Why should I let you into my heaven?'—what would you say?"[2]

Imagine yourself and a partner calling in the home of an unchurched person. During the first ten minutes you would inquire about the family's life and their church background. You would then give a brief description of your own church, followed with a personal statement of what Christ means to you or what being part of the church means to you.

After this brief encounter you would then ask the two questions, which deal with assurance of a relationship with God and the ground of that relation—faith or works.

If the person does not have personal assurance or if that assurance is based on something other than faith in Christ, this deficiency opens the door for a presentation of the gospel of grace.

Having realized that the person does have assurance of salvation, you then present in short sermonic form the gospel of grace to be received through faith.

In the three- or four-minute presentation of the gospel, the witness establishes the fact that all persons need this reconciliation to God because they have sinned. God is holy and just and must punish sin. But because God is also gracious, a way has been provided through Jesus Christ for sinful persons to be forgiven and brought back to God. This salvation must be received through faith, faith alone, and we can do nothing to earn it.

When the gospel has been presented, the witness must bring the individual to a personal response to Christ. Commitment focuses on the desire of the person to be saved, and the guide appeals to the person to make a choice for Christ right now. After clarifying the meaning of commitment, the witness leads the subject in a prayer of commitment and offers the assurance that God hears and answers the sinner's prayer.

Continue this imaginary presentation of the gospel to a stranger at home. Having made a clear presentation of the gospel, you must now bring the person to a decision.

The qualifying question gets the person with whom you are talking to acknowledge the reasonableness of the gospel. *Does that* [the gospel] *make sense to you?*

The commitment question speaks to his or her personal desire: *Do you want to receive the gift of eternal life?*

The clarification question is last: *Would you like to transfer your trust—that is, your hope of getting into heaven—from yourself and what you have been doing to what Christ has done for you?*

Following a positive response to this question, you lead the person in a prayer of commitment, suggest the faithfulness of Christ who is present, and invite the person to trust in him as his or her salvation.

With words of affirmation and gratitude the visit is concluded: you and your partner proceed to visit the next subject for the evening.

If this style of presenting the gospel demonstrates the positive attributes that have been indicated, why has it been looked upon with suspicion and been rejected by so many clergy and lay persons? First, it feels like a "canned" presentation, which serves the same diet to everyone regardless of taste or condition. It lacks the personal application of the gospel to different needs.

Then, to some, this direct, confrontive approach has a brashness about it that intrudes into the privacy of the subject's personal life. "If you died tonight would you go to heaven?" That question is perhaps as personal as saying to a stranger after a few minutes of conversation, "By the way, how is your sex life?"

For others this method of presenting the gospel focuses on a cognitive, volitional commitment rather than the sovereign initiative of the gracious God. True faith is born out of an encounter with the living God.

Finally, this style meets rejection because of its manipulative practices. The closure employs the techniques of a seller of insurance or used cars. This style seems to limit the freedom of the individual while it presumes to control the grace of God.

Certainly these criticisms of confrontational models like that of Evangelism Explosion would be met with explanations and justifications by its advocates, and yet I am convinced that their justifications will not win over the majority of mainline Protestants. The model of spiritual direction for the personal evangelist presented here is offered as an alternative to approaches like Evangelism Explosion, the Four Spiritual Laws, and the Roman Road to Salvation. Our model of a spiritual guide overcomes the confrontational intrusive witness, it presents the gospel in a variety of ways, it does not violate the theological commitments of a postmodern theologian, and it honors the sovereignty of God and the freedom of persons.

The Image of Spiritual Guide

While our description of the reaction to the Evangelism Explosion model may have elements of overstatement, for the most part the evaluation characterizes pastors and laity in mainline Protestantism. As an alternative, we seek in the image of the spiritual director a positive, compelling model that enables one person to share the faith with another in a creative, respectful manner.

Instead of the inquisitive intruder, the image of a spiritual guide suggests two persons on a journey, with one serving as a guide to enable the other to "see sights" that otherwise might go unnoticed. The role of a guide contrasts with that of a researcher, who focuses on data; a judge, who makes evaluations and pronouncements; and an officer, who enforces the law. Guides are participants on the journey; they walk with their companions and stay near them.

The Tasks

Barry and Connolly give a succinct definition of the goal of spiritual direction: "A conscious relation to

God."[3] The spiritual guide seeks to facilitate in persons a consciousness of God by helping them to notice God's action in their lives and respond to it. Out of the immediate awareness of God flows trust and obedience. (Noticing God's action does not always result in obedience; awareness of God may also produce resistance.) What does a spiritual director do? The tasks of the spiritual director must include the following: listening with empathy, paying attention, affirming, clarifying, questioning, and helping the subject become aware. Implicit is the creation of a climate of trust and openness. According to Barry and Connolly, all these tasks "are indispensable to the work of spiritual direction."[4] We intend to exploit the style of the spiritual director for the task of evangelism: that is, to use this style for introducing others to the spiritual journey.

One of the first tasks of the spiritual director is the creation of an atmosphere of warmth, confidentiality, and trust. This environment contrasts with the abrupt intrusion of the "hit-and-run" witness.

Spiritual guides carry an influence within themselves. When they are at peace, when they are warm and gentle, these qualities flow naturally into the relationship with another person. The converse is also true. A rushed, anxious approach breeds the same attitude in the other person.

A positive atmosphere springs from the guide's interest in the subject. Focusing on the interests, experiences, and ideas of the other person has an amazing power to condition the atmosphere. In contrast with a canned approach to evangelism, this style takes the life and experience of the subject with utmost seriousness. When centering attention on the other, the guide lays aside all personal agendas.

When the subject has the full attention of the guide, statements of interest and simple affirmations serve to create a climate of trust. Without trust there can be no effective guidance.

Like the spiritual director, the guide has confidence in

God's power to establish a conscious relationship with godself. When the guide has confidence in God, the pressure to produce a desired response, gain a certain decision, or save a soul eases. The power and the outcome belong to God; we offer ourselves as willing participants in God's intention for that moment.

The effective guide is an empathetic listener. To listen to another, the guide must lay aside his or her personal agenda. Such a divestiture enables the guide to focus on the life experience of the subject and take it seriously. This kind of listening is the basis for genuine dialogue. The tasks of listening can be summed up as listening with one's whole person, listening to the whole person, and listening with gospel filters.

To listen with one's whole person requires listening with eyes, ears, and heart. With our eyes we pay attention to the nonverbal communication of subjects—how they sit, their facial expressions, specific movements, and the evidence of ease or anxiety in their responses. With our ears we listen to their words but we also listen to the meaning behind the words—the tone, the selection, the words they emphasize, the slowness or quickness with which they speak. With our hearts we listen to feelings—the feelings inspired within us and the feelings we imagine they are having.

A good listener listens to the whole person. Can we not see that this posture of empathetic listening casts us into the world of the subject with whom we converse, taking both the subject and his or her world with utter seriousness? As we enter appreciately into the world of another, we listen to the person's past, present, and hopes for the future. Again, this kind of listening emphasizes our understanding the narrative of another's life journey.

A good listener listens through gospel filters. These filters enable us to hear the narrative of another in the context of biblical truth. We listen to the meaning that a person has created for him or herself without reference to God. In one sense life without a conscious relationship with God defines the meaning of being "a sinner."

The gospel filters most helpful for this task are those of "creation," "fall," and "reconciliation." The filter of creation strains out of the narrative "what has made this person the way he or she is": that is, what created this particular person. The filter of the "fall" separates out those parts of a person's narrative that reveal brokenness, emptiness, or alienation—evidences of estrangement from God. "Where are the broken places in this person's life?" The filter of reconciliation seeks to capture those particles of grace which act redemptively in a person's life, tiny vignettes that suggest God's work in a life. "How has God been at work in this person's life?"

Barry and Connolly indicate that one of the major tasks of the director is to "pay attention" to the work of God in another's life. Our description of "listening through gospel filters" fulfills that requirement.

The spiritual guide affirms both the person and the presence of Christ. Without question, affirmation can be as shallow and as manipulative as those aspects of Evangelism Explosion that we have questioned. Thus our affirmations must be genuine.

One Model of Sharing

I once asked each of the participants in a continuing education course to interview one unknown person regarding his or her relationship with God. The request created considerable anxiety, in one man in particular. In spite of his feelings, this man made the effort and reported his experience to the group. He had gone to the hospital hoping to meet someone who was willing to talk. Near the pharmacy in the lobby, he saw a woman in her late twenties reading a magazine. He approached her.

"Hello, do you have a few minutes to talk with me? I'm a seminary student and I'd like to talk with you for a few minutes about faith, if that's okay."

She smiled nervously and squirmed a little. "Yeah, I've got a few minutes, if faith in God is what you mean."

"Yes, that's what I mean."

She smiled. "You just ask the questions, and I'll answer them."

"What can you tell me about your life?"

"I've had a hard life. I've been praying more and more lately. I believe God answers prayers. I've been going to AA, and I've learned to lean on God. I think you can always find God in crisis times. I pray, and he seems to answer my prayers."

The student said to her, "You certainly are an open person. Thank you for sharing so much of yourself with me." Then, feeling the depth of her statement about Alcoholics Anonymous, he asked, "Could you share more of your efforts to pray?"

She said, "I don't know what else to say. I pray, I find strength to leave alcohol alone, and I believe God helps me every day in my life."

In this encounter the seminary student affirmed the value of the person by recognizing her openness. He underscored her awareness of God by asking her to describe how God had been at work in her life.

Another Illustration

An effective guide must also clarify what the other person means. We can too quickly assume that we understand by imputing our meanings to their words. Questions provide one way of clarification.

A minister to young people sought to get one youth involved in a serious discussion about the faith.

MINISTER: "What about Jesus? What do you think of him?"

YOUTH: "He seems a little closer than God, but it's hard to believe some of the things he's supposed to have done. I'm not sure I believe in the resurrection."

MINISTER: "Is the resurrection the major problem for you?"

YOUTH: "Yeah. It's that rising from the dead."

MINISTER: "What part of the resurrection seems most difficult?"

YOUTH: "That he was dead and came back to life. That just doesn't happen."

MINISTER: "If you are going to prove anything, what are the sources you use in order make your point?"

YOUTH: "I guess you have to ask the people who know and then decide if you can trust their answers."

MINISTER: "Do you have any good reason to doubt the witness of men and women who were willing to die for their witness to the resurrection of Christ?"

The effective guide must also become skillful in the use of questions to unearth the story of the person with whom he or she is speaking. I say "skillful" because the unwise use of questions makes the spiritual guide sound like the Grand Inquisitor. Creative questions combined with gospel filters help the guide discover where persons are on their life journey. While the following questions should not be used in a mechanical way, I have found many of them to be good lead-ins for a conversation about faith.

Creation Questions

Could you tell me a little about yourself?
What are some of your earliest memories of good times?
Have you lived in many places?
What was life like for you when you were growing up?
Who were the persons you admired most in your adolescence?

After you have established rapport with a person, you can perhaps ask about deeper areas of need. I have found the following questions helpful.

"Fall" Questions

Do you ever think about the meaning of your life?
Are there times when life just doesn't seem to have any meaning to you?
I find myself wondering, do you have the same kinds of struggles that I do?
Would you be willing to state what you feel your greatest need is?

In the following questions you wish to discover where God is already at work in a person's life. Or you might use these questions to help persons make the connection between their life experience and the presence of God.

Reconciliation Questions

Have there been times in your life when God seemed very near?
Have there been times when you prayed seriously?
Do you think God may have been involved in [an incident they have described]?
What is really important to you? (This tells you what ranks in competition with God in a life.)
Could there have been something more than chance involved in [make a specific reference to an event]?

In all these tasks of the spiritual guide, the central purpose is to help a person become more deeply aware of God. As the guide becomes involved in a person's life, he or she will find the life story reveals both needs and the presence of the Spirit. As the details of a person's life are multiplied, the guide must keep the central task in mind—"to help the subject become aware of God and to respond in obedient faith to this divine presence." Perhaps a story offers the most effective way to clarify a number of our tasks.

I had to go to Chicago. My flight left Atlanta at 7:45 A.M. Because I had a full fare ticket (not discounted), I had the luxury of upgrading to first class for a few additional dollars. As I sank into my spacious first-class aisle seat, I felt a quiet gratitude that the window seat was empty. Out came the book I was reading. Quickly, I was immersed in work. A woman's footsteps in the aisle distracted me momentarily, but she sat down across the way. Thankfully, I kept reading, never so much as looking up from the page. My text spoke of love, servanthood, and sensitivity to the needs of others. I felt a strong stir in my conscience. Troubled by my attitude that I had not wished to be disturbed by the woman who had taken the seat opposite me, I prayed, "All right, Lord, I know my spirit has been wrong. If you wish me to talk with that person, put her in this window seat beside me." I felt both pious and safe—pious in that I had apologized to the Lord and offered myself; safe in the fact that the plane was scheduled to leave in three minutes.

The appointment. In less than a minute, a man, huffing and puffing, stepped through the doorway. He stopped between me and the woman in the adjacent aisle seat. She spoke before the man challenged her.

"Yes, I am in the wrong seat. I belong over there," and she pointed to the vacant seat next to me. With that, she got up, stepped across the aisle, and sat down by the window. I nodded and smiled without speaking.

As my new seatmate got settled, she spoke without provocation. "Are you a minister?" she asked.

"Well, yes, but I didn't know it showed so plainly," I replied.

"Do you want to know how I knew you were a minister?" she inquired.

"I would be interested."

"The way you talk," she said.

Had she overheard me speak to the flight attendant? Or had she heard me checking in before boarding?

"I'm not very religious," she said.

The engagement. With that statement I knew my reading was finished, so I closed the book, placed it in the pocket of the seat before me, and asked, "What do you mean by religious?"

"Oh, attending church, worshiping God, doing the things Christ taught, and giving your money to share in the Lord's work."

As I listened to her definition, I couldn't find much to disagree with. Her notions seemed pretty central to the gospel.

"You don't think of yourself as religious in that way?"
"No."

The exploration. "I would be interested in what stands behind your lack of interest, if you would be willing to talk about it."

She was willing. For the next half hour or more she told me her name was Betty and she was reared a Protestant, a Presbyterian, and then joined the Seventh-Day Adventist Church because her mother was associated with that faith. She described going to a Seventh-Day Adventist school and being taught their strict rules for sabbath and food. As if this legalism was not enough to dampen any soul's interest in religion, she wondered out loud why churches needed so much money, saying that every time she attended worship, the minister was asking for more money. To her, Christianity was "following Jesus and showing love," and love was free. She could not understand the constant pressure for money.

The effort to connect. When the air quieted from this honest attack on institutional religion, I asked Betty, "Do you ever think about God?"

She paused, then answered thoughtfully, "Yes . . . yes, I do."

"I'd be interested in knowing about that," I said.

"I think about God when I have my back to the wall. You know, when things don't go well and you have nowhere else to turn."

I nodded.

"But," she continued, "I feel guilty about calling on God when I'm in trouble, especially when I haven't paid attention to God until I'm in difficulty."

"I really don't think God minds." I sought to encourage her. "God is accustomed to persons getting interested in spiritual matters when life gets tough."

"I also think of God when things are good," she continued. "Sometimes when I get a raise or some new opportunity presents itself, I feel deeply grateful. I need someone to thank, so I thank God!"

Somewhat amused at her self-judgment of being unreligious, I was pondering her statement when she spoke again.

"Then there are times when life seems right. Like when

I'm driving downtown toward the loop, the wind blows off Lake Michigan, the sky is blue and white, fluffy clouds dot the horizon, and I have that feeling of harmony, of being right with myself, in tune with life. God seems so near."

After reflecting a few minutes on what Betty had described as her moments of encounter, I told her, "You don't seem so irreligious to me."

A deeper excavation. She smiled faintly, and we sat quietly a few minutes. I broke the silence. "Betty, do you ever think about the meaning of your life?"

"Oh, yes, ever since I turned thirty-five," she said quickly.

"What sort of answers have you come up with?"

"I don't know. I just don't know. I suppose I won't know the purpose of my life until I have done it. And when I have done what I was born for, I'll die."

The witness. By this time we were landing, and I had no time to explore this last notion of "dying when you have done what you were born for," I said, "God does have a purpose for your life, and to find it is the best thing that can ever happen to you. I hope you will continue to search for it. And remember, let God love you."

The plane was stopping at the gate. Betty stood to depart. As she was leaving, she paused, looked squarely into my eyes, and said, "I'm really going to think about what you have said."

I was moved by this encounter; I felt God had been in that conversation. When I got home, I wrote her a long letter and sent her a little booklet on prayer.

Reflections on Style

While this unscheduled meeting with Betty may not illustrate every aspect of the spiritual director's style, it does incorporate a number of them. Look at this conversation as it models initiative, listening, attending, affirming, clarifying, inquiring, and making the person aware of her resistance.

With respect to initiative, you would have to say that Betty took the initiative. At the outset, I lacked openness or interest in a conversation. My head was on the work I had to do. But something, perhaps God, spoke to me of my preoccupation, self-interest, or whatever stood in the way.

She initiated the conversation by asking if I was a minister. If God had not already gotten my attention by making me aware of my selfishness, certainly her startling statement gave me a clue that an encounter of significance was about to occur.

But when she indicated that she was not "very religious," she opened wide the door to a serious conversation. The initiative of the guide in this instance seems secondary. Yet the sensitivity to hear her call for a listening car is an important characteristic of any guide.

The awareness of this clue points to the importance of empathetic listening. Once the conversation had begun, I became a listener. Listening is the basic posture of the guide. At the outset, the focus was upon Betty—her story, her needs, her questions. What the other person states provides the data which evoke further questions. The story the person tells also indicates the sore spots. When Betty stated that each time she attended church, the minister was always talking about money, she revealed an area of concern. Her description of Christianity as "following Jesus and showing love" further indicated her concept of a faith life.

The guide must attend to the meaning of a person's story. In Betty's story one would conclude rather quickly that religious faith was a matter of concern for her. Did she not ask if I was a minister? Did she not state without my inquiring that she was not religious? The presence of a minister, or someone she thought was a minister, evoked feelings in her strong enough to force these two statements.

Betty very quickly made me aware of the dominant influences in her life. Her mother had been a Presbyterian before she affiliated with the Seventh-Day Adventist Church and sent Betty to a Seventh-Day Adventist school. This information told me volumes about her religious orientation and why she considered herself nonreligious. She meant "not religious like the Seventh-Day Adventists."

There were gaps in the narrative to which I had listened. I knew nothing about Betty's father and the role he played in the shaping of her life. She did not tell me why she occasionally went to church even though she heard only pleas for money. These are but two important gaps of the many which must appear in one brief conversation.

Betty's stated or implied goals were to be successful and happy. When asked about the meaning of her life, she did not readily connect these goals with her purpose for living.

This interview revealed much about the subject's experience of God, most of which was negative. Instead of debating the nature of God, I inquired if she often thought about God. She indicated at least three kinds of times: when she needed help, when she needed someone to thank, when she felt really right with life. Each of these confessions indicated that she was far more religious than she had let herself believe.

In addition to noticing the development of a narrative, the guide affirms the positive aspects of a person's life. Affirmation finds its source of energy in the statement: "For God sent the Son into the world, not to condemn the world, but that the world might be saved through him" (John 3:17). Our task is to affirm and redeem, not to judge and condemn. Jesus' posture with the woman caught in the act of adultery and brought to him for judgment gave a gentle but decisive rebuke to the Pharisees when he said to the woman, "Neither do I condemn you; go and do not sin again" (John 8:11).

When Betty defined her views on religion and related her various experiences of God, I responded, "You seem pretty religious to me." In this context, a positive response carried the weight of affirmation. But perhaps the most affirming response I made was the depth of listening I gave her. Nothing conveys a greater sense of worth to another.

The spiritual guide clarifies the subject's notions. Clarification occurs in three major ways—feedback, questions, and informative statements. By feedback I mean rephrasing what another says so that they may hear their ideas through your lips. I never offered Betty this type of feedback.

A question about the meaning of religion did clarify her negative feelings about the church. Perhaps her response gave me greater clarity than it did her.

During the conversation, I gave very little information. Most of my comments were brief. In other circumstances I might have said more, but this situation seemed to call for listening and gentle response.

Finally, the guide must focus the awareness of the subject. Five common attitudes block the subject's consciousness of God: self-pity, self-sufficiency, low self-esteem, self-delusion, and self-will.

In the first instance persons say that they are too bad for God to be interested in them, and they erect defenses around their consciousness with self-pity.

Some persons claim they are sufficient without God. Their attitude of indifference to God makes the divine Presence of no consequence.

Other persons do not feel any sense of worth; they lack self-esteem. Persons who cannot love themselves find it difficult to believe God or other people can love them.

Others are self-deluded. In some manner, they have acquired misinformation about God, Christ, the church, or the will of God. The misinformation blocks their consciousness.

Still another group blocks the awareness of God through self-will. These persons may have some notion of the will of God, but they do not choose to do it. They prefer their own will to God's.

The major criticism of this style of witness is at the same time its appeal—it often lacks a direct, confrontative challenge to commit oneself to Christ *now*! Yet when God is dealing with a person, there is pressure enough from this initiative to draw the subject into a decisive relation.

This approach to evangelism avoids the hard-hitting, dogmatic, hit-and-run style of other years and offers in its place a truly loving approach to a fellow pilgrim who needs to know the grace of God.

5

A Closer Look at the Person

I don't know where he came from, nor do I know who inspired his diabolical scheme, but I see the success of his endeavors everywhere I go. Who is he?

The prankster! The spectacles prankster! From the nature of his work, he could be another nephew of Screwtape, a brother of Wormwood.

Most anyone can spot his handiwork by taking the time to notice. His most diabolical work consists of distributing spectacles to church people—laity and ministers alike. Once the prankster persuades persons to wear these invisible glasses, they see persons outside the church as monsters. Some look like tigers, others warriors, and still others like hideous creatures from one of the endless sequels to *Friday the 13th.*

When wearing these glasses, each church member reacts the same way—fear of the outsider. Because of their fear, they never approach a friend or a stranger to share the good news of Christ's love. I cannot recall visiting a church where the prankster has not visited and left his distorting lenses.

The visions created by these lenses stimulate wild pictures in the imagination. Those ministers and lay people captivated by these distorted visions imagine that if they were to approach outsiders, these nonparticipants in church would respond, "What concern of yours is my religious life?"

Or, "Will the heathen in Africa go to hell because they never heard of Jesus Christ?"

Or, "If God is loving, why did an earthquake in San Francisco kill all those persons?"

Or, "How can you believe that a man who lived two thousand years ago has anything to say to our generation?"

These unfounded fears of outsiders heighten the wall between the baptized Christian and those who need the church. And as long as persons wear these distorted lenses, the outsider will remain an object of fear and mistrust. Not only will the outsider be lost to the church but those fearful believers will continue to create a culture within the church that perpetuates the stereotype of the outsider.

The distorted vision created by the prankster's spectacles has indeed already shaped the culture of our churches. I see indisputable evidence of this stereotype in the men and women who come to seminary. They are afraid to approach a stranger because they fear negative reactions—"the tiger's growl." While one can understand the power of this cultural influence on seminarians before they come for theological training, you would expect these distortions to be dispelled after a couple of years of study. Unfortunately, such is not the case.

The prankster's work showed up in a recent continuing-education seminar I conducted at a theological seminary. On the first day I introduced the notion that during the seminar, after proper preparation, I wished each of them to have a conversation about personal faith with a stranger. After the assignment the atmosphere became tense and silent.

On the third day when I reminded them that on the following day we would listen to their verbatims, I got several reactions. Some said they could not do the interview; others indicated that they did not consider this task part of the seminar; several remained silent. One particularly sensitive minister said, "I can talk with persons in my congregation, but I simply can't approach a stranger and introduce the subject of religious faith." Since many of these seminar participants had been in the ministry for twenty years or more, I had falsely assumed they would have no difficulty initiating a conversation about personal faith.

To aid the ministry of spiritual guidance, we must take off the spectacles so widely distributed by the prankster. As sensitive, caring people, we need to see more clearly the perspective of persons outside the church. After all, they are the subjects of our evangelization.

Removing the Spectacles

Two things can help us see more clearly, information and experience. Good information about unchurched persons may be the best place to begin. For me, at least, the lenses to my glasses were wiped clean by the findings of Russell Hale, formerly professor of sociology of religion at Lutheran Theological Seminary in Gettysburg, Pennsylvania. I first encountered Russell through his book, *Who Are the Unchurched?* After reading of his experiences in conversing with the unchurched, I wanted to meet him and hear his story firsthand. So I asked him to be an instructor at a Columbia Theological Seminary "School of Evangelism." During the school, he told his story.

Some years ago, he became interested in knowing why persons did not go to church. He received a grant and a sabbatic leave for a year. Before setting out on his journey, he identified six of the most unchurched counties in the nation—Waldo County, Maine; Sarasota County, Florida; Marion County, Alabama; Boone County, West Virginia; Orange County, California; Polk County, Oregon. His goal was to interview the "hard-core" unchurched. To get their names, he went to ministers, priests, and religious leaders and requested them to identify the persons in their community most indifferent to the church. Armed with one question, "Why do you not go to church?" he set out to meet them.

In six months Hale made some amazing discoveries about this sample of the group that constitutes 40 percent of our nation. To a person, these strangers welcomed his call. They eagerly answered his questions. Often they sought to give him gifts or serve him dinner. Occasionally, others would hear about his project and request a visit so they could tell their story. And the persons he visited always thanked him for listening to their stories and for showing so much interest in them.

After six months in the field with the unchurched, Hale sorted through his 165 interviews, which had consumed more than 400 hours. As he reflected on his notes and listened again to the recorded conversations he had had across the nation, he came up with a dozen categories to describe the unchurched. Perhaps a short description of each will help form a clearer picture of that undifferentiated mass about whom the spectacles prankster has deceived us for so long.

The anti-institutionalists. These persons have been offended by the church's preoccupation with itself; they react to the church's demand for money, the support of bureaucratic programs, and the emphasis on tradition rather than people.

The boxed in. These persons have been reared in narrow fundamentalist churches and have experienced the church as oppressive; they have fled the church in order to find space to grow as persons.

The burned out. These persons were found mostly in retirement in Sarasota, Florida. They feel they have done their part for the church; they were loyal members, teachers, leaders in Michigan or Minnesota but now that their children are grown and they are retired, they wish someone else to take responsibility.

Cop-outs. These persons never really got involved with church. Perhaps they attended a worship service or their children attended Sunday school for a time, but they never made a serious commitment.

Happy hedonists. As pleasure seekers, these persons have found so much entertainment in the world that the church cannot compete for their loyalty. Hale seemed to enjoy telling about the young man in southern California whom he caught at 1:30 P.M. between engagements.

"Why do you not go to church?" he asked.

"Well, I'll tell you, I've been surfing in the Pacific all morning, and now I'm headed for the mountains to ski this afternoon. When the church has anything to compare with this life, count me in!"

The locked out. These are persons who do not feel welcome in the church. Some were locked out because of race, culture, or life situation. This group includes divorcées, racially different persons, perhaps those with an alternative sexual preference.

Nomads. Persons on the move represent that part of the population who move every five years. Putting down roots and pulling them up again in a few years has proved too painful, so they have decided to avoid serious commitments.

Pilgrims. These persons are religious tasters, experimenting with a variety of religious experiences. Some were reared in mainline homes and churches but became weary of the dull life of the church. They are testing Eastern religions, yoga, meditation, and even the occult. None feels his or her present religious engagement to be the final one. They are on a journey hoping sometime to find a valid faith.

Publicans. They are so named to contrast with the biblical Pharisees. These persons look upon church members as hypocrites; they consider themselves to be more moral than those within the church.

The Scandalized. These persons wonder, if Jesus Christ is the way to God, "Why are there so many different churches?" They are put off by the scandal of division.

True Unbelievers. These persons simply do not believe in God. Hale found in his sample about the same percentage as that of the Gallup Poll; only about 6 percent of the population claim to be unbelievers.

The Uncertain. These persons do not have a reason for their inactivity in church. Most say, "I just don't know why I don't go to church."[1]

When I heard Russell Hale describe the unchurched and tell his stories about them, especially their responses to his visits, my image of the nonchurched person changed dramatically. Persons outside the church are not the monsters that the prankster's spectacles have caused us to see. They are searching for the meaning of their lives, they have usually had some experience of the church, they have a religious vocabulary and a frame of reference for faith, and in many instances they have been hurt by the church's practice or its failure.

When Hale had concluded his research, he made four important recommendations. He suggested that we should learn to listen. "The overwhelming experience my conversations with the unchurched conveyed to me—the sort of conversation from which I will never recover—was that those outside the churches of America want and need to be heard."[2]

Hale also suggested that we should learn to proclaim the gospel without offensiveness. He acknowledged that the New Testament message has an offense but need not be proclaimed offensively. "If the Christian gospel is an offense to the unbeliever, it is legitimate to ask whether the gospel has in reality been proclaimed and whether the offense may lie in the offensiveness of the proclaimers."[3]

A third plea by Hale involves "understanding the ethos." "The community's spirit or ethos was discernible in the rhetoric. It seems desirable that this spirit be understood and accepted, even if not embraced, by the churches."[4] The community, in part, creates the person; when the church understands the ethos of the community in which it ministers, it more effectively reaches those persons on the outside.

In reflecting upon the data of his interviews, Hale called the church to repent. "Honesty may demand that the churches be reminded of their own need for renewal." Maybe there is something in us as church persons that blocks the communication of the gospel. Hale concluded, "The imperfect moral behavior of Christians is the chief offense the unchurched recognize among the churched."[5]

Character of the Subject

A general characterization will not fit every person we meet. Yet a broad description like the one offered here will provide an idea of what to expect. An identification of the various categories into which persons fall will provide a context for our task of discernment. Consider these four universal characteristics of persons both inside and outside the church.

A Seeker for Meaning

The search for meaning can be seen in everyone's life. This search may not be named; it may even be camouflaged behind defensive screens, yet it motivates all our lives.

This hunger for meaning is nothing less than the disguised search for the will of God. For persons created in the image of God and for God, nothing short of God's will has the power to quench the hunger for meaning. As Gerald May, a psychiatrist who has encountered a number of persons in need, says, "After twenty years of listening to the yearnings of people's hearts I am convinced that all human beings have an inborn desire for God. Whether we are consciously religious or not, this desire is our deepest longing and our most precious treasure."[6]

The hunger for meaning has a past, present, and future aspect.

The Past. Meaning, with respect to the past, can be distorted by guilt, ignorance, and shame. These three issues make the past unacceptable. **Guilt** occurs through real or imagined wrongdoing. Until guilt is resolved, it colors the past and clouds the meaning of one's life. Real guilt, like telling a lie or committing adultery or stealing, while wrong, can be forgiven. Unreal guilt, like false feelings of responsibility for one's parents' divorce, requires a deeper form of guidance.

Sometimes **ignorance**—a lack of understanding or a false perception—blocks the past. A son may feel for years that his dad did not care for him, because he seldom corrected him. Much later he learns that he really didn't need the correction. His fragile self-esteem permitted only gentle rebuke. Meaning in our lives may become questionable when we lack information or have received bad information. Spiritual guidance helps us discern these barriers to faith and thus to meaning.

A third element, ingratitude, may subvert meaning. Ingratitude may, in fact, turn to festering resentment. This negation of a portion of the past may spring from **shame.** Shame means the fear of being exposed. To harbor shame is like having a monster in the basement of your life; considerable energy must be expended in keeping the trapdoor closed lest the monster bound out with destructive rage. Release comes only when we are able to accept our past with whatever failure it contains.

So we may say that the past conditions every person's search for meaning. Guides can facilitate the resolution of guilt through forgiveness, the illumination of ignorance through sharing knowledge, and the acceptance of and gratitude for one's history, which provides for the dissolution of shame.

To clarify these concepts, think of meaning as a stream originating behind us. As it flows from behind, it may contain guilt, ignorance, and ingratitude. These negatives block or distract the flow of meaning in the present. These barriers reside in memory. This suggests that the spiritual guide will be sensitive to the blocks to meaning that flow from a person's past.

When guides seek to help persons begin the journey with God, these barriers from the past often create resistance. So hesitancy on the part of another may indicate an issue unresolved in the past and should not be interpreted as a failure of the guide.

The Present. The search for meaning can be impacted in the present by one's sense of identity, relatedness, and worth. Surely a sense of meaning, in part, grows out of one's **identity.** "Who I am" stands at the center of meaning. The sense of identity in the moment matters greatly if we are to have a settled sense of meaning. How I see myself as a person influences all my life experiences.

Meaning in the present also demands **relatedness—**

who I am in relationship to significant others. Present meaning does not occur in isolation, but in giving and receiving through significant relations. Perhaps solitary confinement causes such deep mental and emotional pain because the jailed one has been cut out of the fabric of relationships.

In our sense of identity, through significant relationships, we must feel a sense of **worth.** We need to be valued and to value ourselves. Feelings of worthlessness certainly undercut the assurance that our lives have meaning.

As spiritual guides, can we not see that sensitivity to a person's needs affects our response? Whether this identity is authentic or feigned, we must begin with who persons perceive themselves to be. An exploration of their relationships with significant others, as well as their sense of personal worth, opens important doors for conversation and reflection.

If we try to visualize the present moment, it is like sitting in a boat on a pond of meaning. The outlet from the pond is a symbol of the future toward which we are moving. The boat in which we sit has a name, an identity; it has connections to other boats on the pond; it has value.

Our meaning is something like the boat on the pond. The water that flows from upstream makes the pond possible; the water is always coming from upstream and passing downstream, but for the moment the particular boat that represents human awareness sits on the pond. Without identity, relatedness, and worth, the boat will sink.

In the present our identity, relatedness, and worth maintain our meaning, so a guide must seek to discover who persons are, how they relate, and how they feel about themselves. These insights come through unforced conversations.

The Future. The search for meaning not only has roots in the past and relatedness in the present but is also affected by expectations of the future, through engagement, movement, and anticipation. Meaning in life must reach beyond the sense of identity, worth, and significant relationships; it demands an **engagement** with the events of one's "lived-in world" through decision and action.

This engagement of our "lived-in worlds," through our work, for example, produces **movement.** A CPA gets the books and audits them; a farmer plants the crop and harvests it; a student studies and takes exams. By engaging their worlds, all these persons create the movement or change that gives life meaning.

Finally, meaning in the present receives its form in part through **anticipation,** expectations of what lies in the future. Like a boomerang, what we hope for in the future rebounds back upon the present. Hopes for the future condition present choices.

Let us return to the image of the stream as a symbol of time. A boat that represents human consciousness sits on the water; it moves with the flow downstream. Yet we do not know what lies around the bend in the river; the boat always moves into the unknown. Let us say that the person steering the boat expects to meet his girlfriend around the next bend in the river. He is therefore willing to engage the rapids and to steer his way through the rocks to reach his goal. His hope for the future gives him courage to take the risks.

Life's meaning has an upstream-downstream character that affects the present through memory and expectation. In all these ways the subject and guide are very much alike—both have the task of making sense out of their lives. They differ in the fact that the guide has come to believe that Jesus Christ offers the meaning of life. In that confidence, certain that the Lord alone discloses the meaning of life, the guide engages the person in the present with the power of Christ.

This search for meaning, which lies at the center of a person's being, is shaped both by the past and the future. Our guidance of persons will always require that we help them come to grips with the meaning of their lives in each of these aspects. So powerful is this drive, I call it a "homing pigeon instinct."

A Creator of a Narrative

In addition to searching for meaning, the other person is the creator of a narrative, the story of his or her life. Persons enflesh the meaning of their lives in narratives, the stories they tell about the lives they have lived.

Since a narrative carries the meaning of our lives, **listening** becomes the most important element in spiritual guidance. In hearing another's story, we hear both the fulfilled and aborted efforts at doing God's will.

My friend Chuck Gerkin provides an enticing and helpful analogy of this narrative-making enterprise. Early in his training experience he heard Antoine Boisen speak of our lives as "living human documents." Our lives compare to a novel, drama, or short story; we carry in our memory the text of our various tabs of meaning.[7]

If the unknown of a person's life resides in the text of that person's story, the guide, to be of help, must ask about the story. After faithful listening, **interpreting** the text of another's story precedes any positive direction.

The process of meaning-making provides yet another perspective from which to listen to another's story. What do we hear from their past—guilt or resolution? Confusion or understanding? Shame or self-acceptance? What do we hear in their present role—confusion or identity? Isolation or relatedness? Worthlessness or self-esteem? What do we hear about the future—withdrawal or engagement? Frozenness or movement? Anxiety or anticipation?

The skilled spiritual guide listens to all aspects of the narrative. The guide wishes to identify, recognize, name, and affirm the positive sides of these polarities and also to note evidence of the negative. Negative experiences often provide the widest doors for change.

If the search for meaning can be symbolized by a "homing pigeon," this narrative aspect makes the subject a "storyteller."

A Bearer of Presence

To speak of the subject as "bearer of presence" is both theologically sound and methodologically effective. This perspective changes the subject from a monster to a bearer of the holy. Quite a contrast! Christ promised that the Holy Spirit would have a universal ministry. The Spirit poured out upon all flesh at Pentecost (Acts 2:17) came to convince, convict, reprove all persons (John 16:8–11). If the Spirit acts upon all persons, this action must be incognito because most of the activity goes unrecognized. So every person we meet has prior experience of God, whether named as such or not. In the deep recesses of the spirit, in the longings of the heart, the subject demonstrates evidence of the work of God's Spirit. Therefore, long before persons name the name of Christ, long before they have a conscious perception of God in the occurrences of life, the divine presence has been speaking, drawing, supporting, and sustaining this person on their life journey.[8]

The fact of God's presence in the life and narrative of the subject assures us of divine assistance in our endeavor. The Spirit has been poured out on humankind; the Spirit has been at work long before we began to participate in this effort, and we can trust that the Spirit will be working when we have finished. No guide takes the Spirit to another; rather, we meet the Spirit already there. How dramatically our approach changes through the recognition that the Spirit has been at work long before we appear on the scene. Responsibility for precipitating a decision and changing another person does not rest on our shoulders but on God. While our lives may be conduits of knowledge or our voices may issue challenges, spiritually transformative work can be done only by God. To trespass in this arena both overloads our capacity and frustrates the grace of God.

Since most persons will be unconscious of the divine Visitor, our role demands a sensitive engagement and gentle questioning to awaken their sleeping spirit. Though the Spirit often works through human needs and hungers, the Spirit also may be hidden in the longings expressed or hinted at in their narrative. Special sensitivity must be given to the past, with its guilt, ignorance, and ingratitude; to the present, with its need for identity, relatedness, and worth; and to the future, with its engagement, movement, and anticipation.

Obviously the conviction of the divine presence in each person's life demands reverence for the individual. Each person made in the image of God, as bearer of the divine presence, and on a sacred journey must be treated with genuine respect. No person has fallen beyond the bounds of this kind of respect. Has Christ not said that when we deal with the least of persons, we deal with him?

A Religious Orientation

Persons in the culture of the United States are characterized by a "religiousness." What does this term mean? Most persons have the rudiments of religious faith. They know the words "God," "Jesus," "church," "Bible," and "salvation." For many in the culture these terms have been corrupted to give a distorted view of the Christian faith; nevertheless, the words can be understood.

Not only do persons outside the church know the vocabulary of faith, many have had "religious" experiences. Ask persons outside the church, "When has God seemed near to you?" Most can give an answer. They will report times of crisis when they have been thrust upon God, or peak experiences that hinted at their life's meaning, or mystical experiences, and some will describe authentic religious experiences.

Most persons in the culture desire to talk about their experiences when they can find a sensitive, receptive hearer. A good listener facilitates a salvific moment. To have an opportunity to tell someone their experience enables them to formulate it more clearly and to discover the meaning of the "experience of God." Good listening offers this opportunity even without any assessment or witness from the guide.

"Religiousness" also manifests itself in beliefs and actions. Most persons in the United States believe in God, think Jesus is more than an ordinary man, and pray on an average of twice a week. Such persons will often respond to an invitation to reconsider the religious dimensions of their life. Many, on the other hand, resist having religious dogma imposed on them. Perhaps they would become more serious religious explorers if more of us were inquirers and listeners.

Like cattle on a Texas ranch, these persons have been branded, "branded by God."

So What?

Earlier I suggested that good information could assist us in working with these persons who have been turned into monsters by the prankster's spectacles. What do the insights of Hale and this deeper look at the unchurched subject suggest to us about spiritual guidance?

Are not these persons more like us than different from us? We share a common humanity, a common drive for meaning, and common failures. Do not these persons possess a kind of faith? They believe life has meaning and seek to create some sense out of their own lives; they carry meaning in a narrative; they have a religious orientation and possess a religious vocabulary; and many have had mystical experiences that they identify as experiences of God.

To change our perception of the outsider, the stranger, we not only need information, we need the catharsis of experience. While experience cannot be packaged and shared vicariously, it does help us to hear of the discoveries of others. The workshop participant who said, "I can speak with members of my church, but I can't speak to a stranger," described the following experience.

I went out for a walk about 10 P.M. As I drew near the graduate college, I recalled that when I was a student I occasionally went to the pub there for a beer. They always had beers from all over the world, and I thought a dark British ale would taste pretty good.

When I arrived at the bar, a sign hung on the door, *de basement bar—this pub for exclusive use of grad school students.*

"I'm not from the graduate college, but I *am* taking a seminar here. Can I still get a beer?" I asked the bartender.

"Sure. We have that sign to keep the undergrads out. What'll you have?"

I ordered their mellow, full-bodied, British ale nicknamed "the Dog." After a while I said, "Are you in the middle of exams?"

The bartender responded, "Some are. Me, I finished my comprehensives last May; now I'm working on my dissertation. Boy! Am I glad to have comps behind me!"

"Why's that?"

"Intense pressure. Unbelievable pressure."

Jokingly, I responded, "You know, when I was a student here I heard stories about grad students jumping from the tower."

"Yeah, they lock the tower during exam time; there's just too much pressure."

"How do students deal with all that stress?"

"Right here in this pub, drinking. Besides drinking, some people exercise."

"Being a minister, I wonder whether anyone finds relief from the strain by turning to religion. Would you say anyone around here is very religious?"

"Oh, yeah. My girlfriend is very religious, but I'm not. I used to be but not anymore."

There was a break in the conversation while he waited on customers. After a period of silence the student bartender spoke.

"My dad's a minister—Lutheran. I grew up in church, went to Sunday school, youth groups, the whole thing. Lately, I've lost interest."

"Why is that?"

"My girlfriend and I talk about it a lot. She's Catholic and very religious, and she wonders why I don't go to church much anymore. I'm not sure, really."

There was another interruption.

Without any inducement the bartender picked up the conversation again. "I was in Charlotte this weekend and went to church. It was weird to sit in the pew and listen to my dad preach."

He remarked that his parents were divorced and he lived with his mother.

"It was good to be back, good to sing the hymns. But you know what got to me? Saying the Nicene Creed. As I was saying it, I said to myself, 'I don't believe this stuff anymore.'"

"In what field are you writing your thesis?"

"Physics, why?"

"I was just wondering whether the kind of mind it takes to do physics seems incompatible with things of faith."

"No, that's not the issue for me. I know some people who can put the two together very well. I believe God is out there, just not very interested. I don't know why I'm so indifferent."

After a third interruption, the bartender resumed. "Physics is so precise. We look for measurable things; we discover; we search."

Another interruption.

"I've been thinking about what you said about the searching part of physics," I said. "I wonder whether you've ever thought of religion in the same way—that religion may not be as straightforward as reciting the Nicene Creed. Maybe it's like physics, a search, an effort to discover God here and there in the places you and I might not think to look unless we were searching."

The bartender looked intrigued. "I've never thought about religion or God that way before. Let me think about this."

Would you say this experience dissolved some fears the student may have had?

6

A Faith-Awareness Spectrum

Perhaps a change of spectacles will not be enough; a reading lens may be necessary. The prankster, through devious methods, distorts the perception of faithful Christians to scare them away from outsiders. Even when sensitive, caring church members have been stripped of their distorted spectacles, something else is needed—a close-up lens. These additional lenses function like bifocals to help the guide see more clearly the outsiders' awareness of God.

Let us say that we have been disabused of our fear of outsiders and truly wish to engage them in a significant encounter. How shall our inquiring eyes see the activity of the Spirit in the narrative of the subject? This question demands that we explore more deeply the religious dimension of a person's narrative and of that individual's awareness of God. To assist in this discernment we will provide a spectrum of religious consciousness; the type of consciousness in the subject provides the starting point for the spiritual guide. To help a person become conscious of Christ and to respond to that person is, after all, what evangelism is all about.

Types of Human Consciousness

Both evangelistic witness and spiritual guidance focus on human consciousness. In consciousness, our transactions with God occur. In primary spiritual guidance the guide endeavors to help the subject become aware of the invitations of Christ to a relationship. This initial awareness goes by many names: repentance, conversion, justification, regeneration. Repentance means "turning" from one thing to another—like turning from self to God. Conversion has the same root meaning: to convert means to shift one's perspective. Justification has the atmosphere of a courtroom in which one has been declared right; through faith God declares our past forgiven and our person accepted. Regeneration, new birth, speaks of the beginning of new life. Whatever the metaphor, each describes a moment of conscious response to God, the acceptance of forgiveness, or the gift of divine presence; all these moments mark the beginning of an intentional life with God.

Spiritual guidance aims to develop or expand this consciousness of God. The work of guiding another occurs on a very fine line between divine sovereignty and human agency. No guide has control over the initiative of God, but God chooses to use such persons to mediate the divine presence. Those who need the grace of God can make no claim upon God, but God continuously comes to them, seeking their response. True change consists of nothing but a response to divine initiative: God acts, humans respond. I am quite sure that when persons find themselves searching, praying, hoping for help from God, they do not read their efforts as a response to divine initiative. Only later do they "see" God as the initiator of their quest. In this light the spiritual guide helps a person notice the initiatives of God and respond to them. Calling attention to resistance to these divine initiatives may also be another part of the task.

Our investigation of forms of consciousness will be aided by the creative concepts of Carl G. Jung, the Swiss psychiatrist. He provides a perspective on human consciousness informative of our task.[1]

Jung recognized three aspects of the human psyche: consciousness, personal unconscious, and collective unconscious. By **consciousness,** Jung meant the zone of immediate awareness: this room where I sit, the television to my left, the sound of the pen scratching on the paper, the open curtain and the world outside—in succession, these different images are the focus of my personal consciousness. By the **personal unconscious,** Jung meant those past experiences, positive and negative, held in memory, the untapped potential of one's life, the shadow side of one's being, the dark, mysterious side that sometimes breaks out in destructive acts. He also included the subjective aspects of the function of consciousness and the control of involuntary bodily functions in the personal unconscious. By **collective unconscious,** Jung intended the notion of a racial memory, the domain of archetypes and symbols that play key roles in the myths of all cultures. For the purpose of initial spiritual guidance our focus centers on consciousness and the personal unconscious.

In our discussion of the triadic faith structure we have indicated that from the moment of birth the divine Spirit functions unconsciously in our lives. Long before persons consciously experience the presence of God, the Spirit has been creating hungers in them. These hungers can only be satisfied through a relationship with the divine; so, if heeded, they would through frustration and fulfillment lead persons to recognize their helplessness without Christ. In all that the Spirit does, the Spirit seeks to draw persons to Christ by conviction, by reproof, by enlightenment, and by the truth. The Spirit aims to make subjective in personal experience what Christ has done objectively through his death and resurrection. Paul had in mind this experiential unity with Christ when he said, "For if we have been united with him in a death like his, we shall certainly be united with him in a resurrection like his" (Rom. 6:5). The Spirit creates this subjective identification.

How does the awareness of the Spirit enter human consciousness to create this inner transformation? Jung describes two ways, by intuition and by sensation: that is, from the inside through ideas and inspirations and from the outside through sensory experience.

Intuition. The thought of God comes into consciousness at times through flashes of insight, hunches, creative vision—experiences that may be inspired by the Spirit. Though it would be absurd to identify every intuition with the Spirit, surely it would be just as unwise to hold that the Spirit never comes through revelatory intuitions. These experiences of intuition may represent the Spirit's redemptive work even in those who know nothing about the Spirit.

In the case of the uninformed, these revelatory moments do not hold lasting significance but slip back into the unconscious like a dream that cannot be remembered the morning after. Positive intuitions require naming and nurturing. But in persons with religious training, the Spirit often speaks to consciousness through intuitions. The intuitions can be grasped, held, and acted on through the language of faith. A friend of mine, a member of the church but not too obedient, tells about buying a pint of vodka, half of which he consumed while driving home from a neighboring town. As he drove down the highway, a voice spoke in his head: "Jack, stop drinking; see your doctor." He felt compelled to listen to the intuition. He saw his doctor, got treatment, and was cured. From that day to this, he has not had another drink; he has been changed in his outlook, lifestyle, and values. He recognized the intuition as the voice of God because he had the symbols with which to name and respond to the Spirit.

Sensation. Ideas also come to consciousness through sensation—the use of the five senses. While the spiritual guide should be aware of the assistance of the Spirit through intuitions, the guide manipulates neither the Spirit nor the intuition. The various efforts of the spiritual guide occur in consciousness through the subject's perception of the guide. For example, asking persons about themselves, being seen as a listener, feeding back to the subject elements of his or her story—all these initiatives occur in consciousness through actions that stimulate one of the five senses. Obviously, the preaching of the gospel and personal witness enter consciousness through seeing and hearing.

The miracle of revelation, or salvation, occurs when the Spirit in the unconscious depths of the psyche unites a person's consciousness with Christ. Persons describe the experience as conversion, being born again, or personally meeting Jesus Christ. Or the Spirit may function from the outside through the medium of the guide, the scriptures, or a revelatory event in the life of the subject to create this new relationship with God. By whatever medium, whether through intuition or sensation, initial spiritual guidance aims at a new center of consciousness created by an encounter with Christ.

A Spectrum of Consciousness

As the spiritual guide listens to the narrative of another, one question must be uppermost: To what extent is this person aware of Christ? To assist in this task, I will describe a spectrum of awareness, which begins in the dark of unawareness and moves toward the clarity of a Christ-centered consciousness. The descriptions of each type will be more suggestive than exhaustive; the types are not pure, but they serve in a general way to assist the spiritual guide in discerning the spiritual state of the subject.

With respect to an awareness of God, human consciousness can have at least five types of content. Probably each has a mixture of other types. The "unaware" person may possess some awareness of God, but not enough to evoke a response or consciously influence the person's life. The person who is unconscious of God, when impacted by the Spirit, experiences a change in consciousness. Our purpose will be to describe each mode of consciousness and how it relates to scripture, provide responses that may be helpful, and give a specific illustration of each type.

Unawareness

Some persons seem to be totally unaware of God. These persons live without consciously identifying the presence of God in their lives; they do not give serious thought to God; they manifest no interest in a religious faith or life. These persons often appear to be restless, constantly seeking fulfillment through achievement or pleasure. Sometimes they focus their full attention on a job, which for a time offers integration and meaning. Yet the dominant characteristic of these persons seems to be life without awareness of God.

Jesus described the consciousness of these persons as soil "by the way side" (Matt. 13:4, KJV) into which the seed does not penetrate. He spoke of them as having eyes which do not see and ears which do not hear. Their problem issues not from a lack of ability but from the nonuse of those abilities.

Paul described this mode of consciousness with the metaphor of death. He said, "And you he made alive, when you were dead through the trespasses and sins in which you once walked" (Eph. 2:1–2). Through sin, the capacities for fellowship with God have ceased to function. In some respects they are like a portable radio that has all its parts in good working order but cannot pick up the signal because the batteries are dead.

The following story will illustrate this state of deadness.

A chaplain had been asked to visit an officer's brother in the hospital. The ill person, in his mid-forties, had been diagnosed as having terminal cancer. Some years before, this man had rejected all faith in God, and he had refused to talk about the matter since discovering his malignancy.

The chaplain went for a visit, made a few remarks, and expressed his concern for the patient. At one point he said, "Your brother told me the cancer is worse than you first thought."

"Yeah. I had some hope, but now I just can't find any."

"Feel pretty frightened, huh?"

"Yes, and I'm sure Dick has told you that God has not been real to me for a long time, so prayer can't do much good for me."

"He told me, but I am sure that you know I believe God can help you."

"I studied Christianity and the other religions, and I've come to believe that God is a myth people created because they needed a crutch. Even if God existed, he couldn't answer everyone's prayers."

"I know you have figured that out in your head, but what does your heart tell you?"

"I used to believe God answered prayer and that Jesus Christ was our Savior—that's the way I was raised. When I began studying other faiths, I came to the conclusion that all people are trying to find answers to questions for which there are none. God just seems to be an easy way out."

"If God were smaller, you could believe in God? If you knew everything about God, could you have faith?"

"No. I think there must be some mystery there. My problem is I just don't see God at work in the world—there's too much pain and suffering."

The chaplain felt it time to make his statement. "I think all of us have wished at some time for God to give us a clear demonstration, and I believe God did just that in

Jesus Christ. He didn't answer all our questions, but he did show us God's boundless love and he offered us hope."

The Spirit seemed to use those words of witness and comfort. The man with cancer responded, "Facing what I am, I really want to believe that God is real, that Christ can save me, and there is a heaven. I have rejected the idea so long I can't just say words, I have to mean them."

"In your heart and not just in your head?"

"Yes."

"Jim, I believe your desire is a good, first step back to Christ. Accept this new desire as the small beginning of faith and your journey has begun."

"I wish it were that easy!"

"It is. It is!"

The chaplain sought to make this person aware of God, to help him begin thinking of God as one who cared for him. What can one person do to make another person aware of God? In the final sense, nothing. "Only God reveals God." But in the midst of this conversation it appeared that a desire for God was awakened both through the positive memories of the patient and the witness of the chaplain. After the chaplain had given witness to his faith, the man said, "Facing what I am, I really want to believe that God is real." Do we not believe the Spirit of God inspired the desire for faith that lies behind this confession?

Cultural Religious Awareness

A large segment of those persons whom we encounter will be religiously informed by the culture. In our previous discussion of the "religiousness" of the American population we discovered that many persons have the rudiments of faith. According to a Gallup Poll, 94 percent of the general public believe in God, 92 percent state they pray several times each week, and almost 86 percent believe that Jesus was more than an ordinary man. These rudimentary beliefs and practices, despite the chosen lifestyle of the persons involved, suggest that a large percentage of the population has a general faith.

Perhaps this consciousness may be illustrated in Ed Allen's reaction. My predecessor at the small village church had visited Ed in his home, hoping to interest him in the church for the sake of Ed's wife, who attended worship regularly.

In the course of the visit, the pastor asked, "Mr. Allen, are you a Christian?"

His reply came quickly, a typical cultural response. "Hell, yes, what do you think I am, a pagan?"

Perhaps Jesus had this group in mind when he spoke of the tares among the wheat. Tares sprout with the wheat; they look like wheat, they produce like wheat, but they are not wheat.

In the United States, these masses of persons engage in a religious life of their own making. They have the language and symbols of religious faith, but these symbols point to a vague form of religion or a privatized religion of self-interest. Knowledge of the true God and the demands of responsible obedience are far removed from the consciousness of these persons.

In New Testament days the publicans approximated this group of persons. The publicans were renegade Jews who had sold out to the Roman establishment. They deemed a relationship to Rome to be in their own best interest and therefore turned away from the faithful practice of their faith. Despite their disobedience to the law and their desertion of the Temple, they retained the rudiments of Judaism.

Can you imagine a conversation between Jesus and Zacchaeus as they made their way to the host's home?

"Come down from your perch in the tree, I wish to have lunch with you."

"Me? A publican?"

"Yes. You are a child of Abraham, aren't you?"

"I suppose so. But . . . but I've not practiced the faith for so long."

Around the table the conversation continues.

"When my Father chose Abraham, he chose you. You are of the seed of Abraham."

"You mean my neglect and downright disobedience do not cancel out that choice?"

"My Father's choice was never dependent upon your trust or obedience, only upon divine mercy."

"Could there be hope for me?"

"Certainly. Abba loves you, wants you, and generously offers you a place among the people."

"Mercy. I've wished I could find my way back. Why, I'd give half of my earnings to the poor if I could find my faith. If I have taken anything falsely, I'll restore it fourfold."

Or consider one of the modern publicans, a Zacchaeus of our day. Keith is a friend of Richard's. They belong to a civic organization and find themselves sharing work projects. After working on one of these projects, Richard engages Keith in a conversation that illustrates this "cultural religious consciousness."

"Keith, I'm curious. May I ask you a personal question?"

"Sure."

"I know we've been friends for a long time and have been through a lot together . . . but I've never asked you about your faith."

"Not much to tell. You know I don't go to church."

"I'm more interested in your faith than your church attendance. Are there times when you think about God?"

"I pray sometimes. I ask for help. Sometimes I wonder how he can let some things happen!"

"Like what?"

"Do you remember that little Wilson girl? Her family's car was hit head on by a drunk driver and she was killed instantly. I wanted to beat that bastard to a pulp. That night I seriously wondered if there was a God."

"I know what you mean."

"I just don't understand why such bad things happen."

"You said that you pray. Does God listen?"

"Yes, he listens. I wish he'd answer like I want, but I suppose he knows best."

"Sounds like you've got some faith to me."

"I guess so, but most people say that to be a Christian you have to say certain things . . . don't do other things

. . . and believe a long list. I can't hang in there with that stuff."

"I'd be interested in knowing what it means to you 'to be a Christian.' "

"It means living right, helping your neighbor, not gossiping. Boy! I can't stand that. Folks claiming to be a Christian and stabbing you in the back."

"Though you don't go to church, from what you are telling me I get the impression that God is important to you."

"Yes, he is."

"And do you think you're important to God?"

"I hope so."

"I believe you are. I believe that you are important to God, and you certainly are important to me."

Keith possesses all those elements of the culturally religious: he knows about God, he prays, he hopes for God's interest. He has little interest in the church and criticizes the members for their hypocrisy. Richard found him both willing and able to talk about his faith. Would not this initial conversation open the door to more serious talks in the future?

Two words of caution: first, leaders in the church may interpret our efforts with publicans, prostitutes, and sinners as a moral compromise. The spiritual guide's sense of identity and integrity must be strong enough to withstand this criticism. Second, the spiritual guide must not be duped by the selfishness of the culturally religious. If they act with expediency regarding Rome, they will do no less with Jerusalem. The spiritual guide will probably need to help these persons purify their cultural faith with a biblically informed faith.

Traditional Religious Awareness

In a ministry of spiritual guidance, the guide will meet many persons who have a belief in God and perhaps hold to the tenets of the Christian faith. These persons have been baptized, reared in Christian homes, and instructed in the faith. Some may have attended church with regularity; they can repeat the Apostles' Creed and The Lord's Prayer. But though they are children of the church, their experience of the faith is often shallow and superficial; they have not experienced in their own life the meaning of the faith they confess.

In many ways this traditional consciousness reminds us of the Pharisees—a strong, clearly defined religious framework without the dynamic power of the Spirit. Jesus said to these persons, "You cleanse the outside of the cup and of the plate, but inside they are full of extortion and rapacity. You blind Pharisee! first cleanse the inside of the cup and of the plate, that the outside may also be clean" (Matt. 23:25–26). Paul warned about those persons "holding the form of religion but denying the power of it," saying, "Avoid such people" (2 Tim. 3:5).

Chuck grew up with Ken; they were close friends. Each had pursued his own vocation. Chuck became a minister, Ken a doctor in a small town. Chuck began the conversation.

"Ken, we've known each other a long time, but I've never talked with you about what I think is the most important thing in a person's life. In some ways I guess I've been afraid it would hurt our friendship."

"What's that?"

"I've never asked you about your faith. What do you believe about God? About Jesus Christ?"

Ken responded immediately. "No reason to be afraid. In fact, I'm glad you asked. I've wanted to have a serious discussion with you ever since I heard about your going into the ministry. Somehow I felt you might help me, but I didn't know how to bring it up."

Chuck felt the pinch. "Isn't that strange. Here I am a minister, and I'm afraid to talk with my best friend about the most meaningful thing in my life!" He paused. "Well, Ken, tell me about your faith."

"You know me. I've always been part of the church. My folks saw to that. I just don't think the God of the church got in me. Isn't that odd? Here I am a religious person and not really religious at all. I guess I'm going through the motions; it seems the right thing to do for family, tradition, friends, social relations, and business. Being in the church, doing the right things but for no good reason. What do you think?"

"I think it is possible to have form without content, to have a body of beliefs without the spirit of faith. Somehow, I think your admitting where you are, owning up to it, is very important."

"I guess religion to me has always been a formal thing. You know, you inherit it from your family, borrow it from friends, marry into it, or adopt it. Around here, going to church is a mark of respectability; it's the fashionable thing to do."

"Ken, I hope you'll reflect on what you've said. If you are willing, admitting these things to yourself could mark the beginning of an important search for a vital, personal faith."

In this encounter Chuck tried to help his friend experience what he already believed. I met one of these persons years ago. He told me all the things he believed. When he finished commending himself to me, I said, "But Bill, has this changed your life?" Years later he told me this was a key question for him. The guide must neither be deceived nor put off by a show of religion in this type of person. It is essential to deal both with personal commitment and change.

Encounters with persons like Bill and Ken remind me of a penetrating statement I read somewhere; I believe it was made by John Westerhoff. "The greatest challenge facing the church today is in the bland, ignorant, unconverted lives of its adult members; until adults in the

church are knowledgeable in their faith, have experienced the transforming power of the gospel, and live radical lives characteristic of the disciples of Jesus Christ, nothing else matters." Many of these persons need to be evangelized.

A Spiritually Awakened Consciousness

If we are successful in our efforts with the unaware, the cultural, and the traditional, each will in some manner be awakened. This awakening may be gradual or dramatic. In the first case, it will be an interruption, and in the second a shattering, of consciousness. As they are confronted by Christ, persons begin to recognize the emptiness of their lives and the inadequacy of their view of life. This awareness produces anxiety and drives them to ask for answers to life that lie outside their capabilities to find.

We recognize this concern in Nicodemus, a man who came to Jesus saying, "Rabbi, we know that you are a teacher come from God; for no one can do these signs that you do, unless God is with him" (John 3:2). Immediately Jesus recognized the state of this man's soul and spoke directly to it. "You must be born anew," he said. Other examples of awakening can be cited in scripture: the rich young ruler, Simon the Pharisee, Saul of Tarsus, the man who said to Jesus, "I will follow you wherever you go."

What do awakened persons need? First, they need someone who can listen. The structure of their lives has been threatened and has sometimes begun to come apart. The experience is painful but good; new life cannot emerge until the old life has come unglued. A good listener lets them unload their anxiety. Once they have shared themselves, the spiritual guide may need to supply information or issue a clear invitation of commitment to Christ. The spiritual guide may be called upon to speak in the place of Christ: "God loves you; God accepts you; your sins are forgiven."

I think the spiritual guide must be cautious not to push for resolution too quickly. An awakened soul may need to engage in spiritual struggle; this struggle becomes part of the re-creative process. To offer encouragement and the truth of the Lord will be good, but to offer assurance before a person has been fully grasped by the Spirit of God will prove disruptive, like helping the butterfly out of the cocoon prematurely, which causes it to die.

Special services were announced at the church. A college student showed up two hours before the worship was to begin. One of the members, Peter, approached the sanctuary and noticed the young man sitting on the steps.

"My name is Peter," he said.

"I'm David. I'm a student at the college, and I came over for the service this evening."

"Glad you did, but are you aware that the service is not until seven-thirty?"

"Yes. I just needed some time to think, so I came over to sit for a while to try to settle my thoughts."

"Would you join us for dinner? We're serving in about forty-five minutes."

"Sure. Cafeteria food is terrible."

"Come on over to the parlor. It will be more comfortable, and we can talk a bit before dinner is served."

In the next fifteen minutes Peter discovered that David lived on the coast, he was a freshman, his parents operated several businesses, and he was the youngest of five children and a drama major.

At one point David said, "I'm not really concerned about the Christian faith, I don't think. I was lonely and had some questions. I heard that when students come here, the church really accepts them."

Peter said, "That makes me feel good. We do try to be responsive to the students when they come. . . . You said that you were lonely—feeling homesick? Missing your family?"

"In a way. But I seem to be lonely in general. In the world I seem to be lost or out of step, perhaps forgotten."

Peter wanted to be perceptive. "Do you think this is a sense of separation from God?"

David paused a long time. "I do feel a distance from God. It is like I want to know more about God, but I am on one side of a cliff and God is on the other—I can't reach across the gap."

"David," Peter said, "God's gift to us is Christ; God has reached across that gap for all of—"

David interrupted before Peter had finished. "I am not pious. I do a lot of stuff that the church does not like. I do things that displease my parents. My dad thinks being a drama major and not a business major is wrong. My dad even thinks that all drama majors are gay. How can you get close to God when nobody accepts the way you are?"

What now needs to be said to David? Does not David give a rather clear indication that some things in his life are bothering him, things that keep him from feeling close to God? Must he not hear that God loves him? Does not Peter have to show him that God is not like his earthly father, who cannot accept him as a drama major? Is David troubled with homosexual feelings?

A New Center of Consciousness

An effective invitation to the awakened might be to "give as much of yourself as you can, to as much of Christ as you understand." Persons cannot give what they cannot give; to give or surrender what they can breaks the log jam and permits commitment to grow. The attitude of "willingness" places a person in a receptive posture rather than a defensive one. "To as much of Christ as they understand"? Persons can only respond to the information they have. More, they cannot do.

To a person like David who has been encountered by the Spirit, we extend an invitation to receive the grace of God, to turn to God in gratitude. In that event of awareness and response, a new center of awareness has been created—an awareness of Christ. This new sense may come gradually into consciousness, like a submarine that has been skimming the ocean floor and slowly surfaces. Or it may come like a flash of lightning on a dark night, illuminating the mind with an experience of God that explains the past and conditions the future.

The New Testament has many metaphors for this mode of consciousness: new birth, a new creation, alive, raised from death, justification, or the experience of being called by God. All these symbols point to a new relationship with God, one that alters the old consciousness, which has been dead, dull, or blocked by conflict.

How do we help someone who has had such an awakening? Another experience may help. I met Joanne a few years ago on a retreat. By accident, we had breakfast together and seemed to get immediately into a conversation about her life.

She wondered, "If I commit myself to Christ, will there be anything there? Will Christ be real and present to me?"

I offered her a few words of assurance. That evening during the address, when I looked into Joanne's face, I saw a radiance that flowed from joy. After the session, I asked her what had happened. She explained that she had turned her life over to Christ; she believed he had taken control.

In the months that followed, I wrote numerous letters in response to her queries. On one or two occasions over the next two years, I had face-to-face exchanges with Joanne while on visits to New York. As a serious Christian, she began to be plagued by the issue of her vocation. And God, to her, seemed to work very slowly.

Much to my surprise, and I think to Joanne's also, she began to feel a call to ministry. With fear and trembling she enrolled in seminary and began her studies. In the new center of consciousness she discovered Jesus Christ, the answer to her life.

A newly constructed person needs someone to talk with. In sharing with another, the new identity becomes clearer. Such a person often needs support and reassurance, like a child taking those first steps. A few suggestions about prayer and Christian literature to read usually prove helpful. The spiritual guide serves in these roles.

7

The Role of Discernment

By this time anyone desiring to be an effective spiritual guide must surely be concerned with discernment. How can we sense the work of the Spirit in the life of another? Times of crisis and periods of transition mark the point when persons are most open to changes in their lives. The crises of death, personal loss, a physical move, or a job loss disturb our modes of consciousness and create a willingness to consider other life options. Those predictable periods of transition—adolescence, going to college, having a child, the last child leaving home, and retiring—also create an environment for change.

The literature on spiritual direction emphasizes discernment as a central task of the spiritual guide. The word "discernment" means to distinguish or to judge between two different things. In initial spiritual guidance, discernment requires us to distinguish the context of the subject, the need being experienced, the presence of God, and the most helpful response. All Christians have a degree of discernment, but mature discernment requires time and experience.

Eyes to See

Discernment requires a special perception, a conditioned vision that enables us to "see" the evidences of

God's activity in another's life. Some years ago, one of the soft drink companies sponsored a television program that could be viewed in three dimensions with the help of a special pair of glasses. By purchasing a six-pack of soda, you received a free pair of 3-D glasses with which the television presentation could be experienced in three dimensions. Persons without the glasses saw a flat two-dimensional movie.

These special lenses point toward an aspect of discernment: the ability to see what does not appear to the unaided eye.

According to Paul, this ability to see is a gift of the Holy Spirit. "To one is given through the Spirit the utterance of wisdom, . . . to another the ability to distinguish between spirits" (1 Cor. 12:8, 10b). So this capacity in spiritual guides has a deeper foundation than their own natural ability. All believers have the Spirit, and their ability to discern comes through the Spirit. Some persons seem to have a particular gift for recognizing the activity of God, a gift extremely valuable to a spiritual guide. Though a gift, this special faculty can also be acquired and developed.

An Illustration

One fertile opportunity to guide parents comes at the baptism of a child. It is a natural transition; it is a time parents reconsider their roles. To set forth the issues in discernment we will examine one pastor's prebaptismal visit. The parents had asked Frank Jackson to baptize their first child; he saw this as an opportunity to share the faith with them. Both parents had been reared in the church but had been inactive for several years. Following the death of his father, the husband had returned from abroad to run the family business.

The minister felt anxious and unsure of his discernment during the visit with the parents. Afterward, the minister reflected, "I felt frustrated that I could not get to more basic issues of faith with the couple." He admitted that he talked entirely too much and felt that he did not share much of the gospel. He left feeling there was a wall between him and the couple, and he wished he could have shared more of his own faith. He wondered how he could have drawn out their story in a more effective manner. We will examine the report of his visit to determine how a more sensitive discernment could have enhanced his approach to the parents.

Frank arrived at the home of the couple and was invited in by Ralph. He noted Matthew asleep in a baby carrier on the floor; he greeted Linda. After a response from both parents, he began a conversation about the baptism.

"Why do you wish to have Matthew baptized? Don't feel put on the spot, but just state your reasons as clearly as you can." Looking at both of them, he waited for a response.

After a long pause Linda spoke. "I think we want him baptized so that he can get started in church."

Frank said, "Baptism is our entrance into the faith and the manner in which most of us get into the church, isn't it?"

He paused, but there was no response.

The minister continued. "We affirm our faith on important occasions by asking questions of each other. Do you affirm your own faith in Jesus Christ as Savior and Lord?"

They both nodded affirmatively.

"Your faith in God is most important. Would you say that you have always been 'convinced' Christians, or are you 'on the way' to real conviction about your faith?"

Ralph answered haltingly. "Well . . . we kind of got uninvolved during college, but the older you are . . . and with Matt coming along we're beginning to get back."

"Good. Now, the second question: 'Do you claim God's covenant promises on your child's behalf?' Can you think of any covenant promises?" Both were silent. The minister explained the meaning of a covenant, something of God's promise to Abraham and the fuller promise in Christ.

When he asked if they had any questions, they shook their heads, indicating they did not.

"The third question is: 'Do you now unreservedly promise, in humble reliance upon God's grace, to set before Matt an example of the new life in Christ?' How would you describe this 'new life in Christ'?"

Ralph spoke first. "Well, it's the whole thing about faith and taking the family to church."

His wife joined in. "It has a lot to do with respecting other people and being a good citizen."

"Yes, that's true," the minister said. "You both have some key ideas, the main ideas. Can you say more about how this new life happens in the home?"

"Forgiveness. And, of course, faith," Ralph said.

Linda added, "The forgiveness of our children when they do wrong."

Frank pressed on with his agenda. "Well, finally, 'Do you promise to pray with and for Matt and to bring him up in the knowledge and love of God?"

"Yes."

The minister then explained the importance of having Matt in the community of faith where his learning could be encouraged by others. He also gave witness to the faithfulness of his own parents in taking him to church.

When the minister finished, Ralph said, "So this is more for us than it is for Matthew?"

"In a way, but Matthew is certainly involved also. And the church joins you in these responsibilities."

The minister covered several particular details about the service, had prayer, and departed.

A Reflection

This encounter between pastor and parents offers several insights regarding the need for discernment. Frank realized that his effort had been ineffective. How could he have engaged the parents in a more helpful way?

The minister had an agenda—to review the baptismal questions with the parents. When he asked their reason for baptizing Matt, if he had been discerning, he would have seen their uncertainty and their need for information and personal guidance. When he asked them to affirm their own faith, they showed further signs of hesitancy and uncertainty. The minister seemed not to notice; if he did, his own anxiety seemed to drive him on. He asked a difficult question: "Can you think of any covenant promises?" Naturally, they could not. Because of their silence, both he and they were embarrassed. With the press of time, the awkwardness of the situation, and the fragile contact that had previously been established, the minister pressed on with his agenda, prayed, said "good night," and went home with a feeling of emptiness and a longing to have been more effective.

In light of what we have already discovered about persons, how could the time have been spent more fruitfully? Perhaps the interview would have gone differently if the minister had discerned the faith experience of the parents and had then discerned the gospel truth for the occasion.

A Process of Discernment

Granted that the minister could have been more perceptive in his visit with these parents, how should he have proceeded? What questions should he have asked? What criteria should he have used to evaluate the data coming to him? If he had asked himself about the couple's mode of consciousness, perhaps he would have responded differently. If he had listened through "gospel filters," perhaps that would have given him clues for his conversation.

Suppose the minister had wondered about the mode of consciousness of this couple. Do they not have a traditional religious consciousness? They know the words of the church—faith, prayer, forgiveness—but they exhibit little if any personal knowledge of the faith. What does this imply for Frank as he counsels them regarding the baptism?

If he had been listening through faith filters, how would they have affected his hearing? The filters of creation, fall, and reconciliation would have helped him sift out several important elements in their faith. From the brief conversation with this couple, several factors in their creation appear. They indicated a church upbringing, which implies a certain view of the world, a set of Christian values, and a notion of God. In addition to the information shared by the couple, the minister knew that Ralph had a positive role model in his father, who had been an elder for years, and that Linda was the daughter of a minister. While the couple did not indicate a response to their rearing, a few personal facts add to the minister's understanding.

What evidence of "fallenness" occurs in their conversation? If the minister listens carefully, he notes that they moved away from the teaching of their families when they went to college. Their conversation centers on Matthew rather than themselves and lacks a sensitivity to the faith. Their "turning away," "shallow interest," and "unfamiliarity" with the centralities of the faith suggest a degree of alienation from God.

With sensitive ears the minister also hears this couple indicate where God is at work in their lives. First, they have asked him to baptize their baby, a decision that indicates a religious concern. They want Matthew to "get started" in the church. Maybe their desire to have Matthew baptized marks the beginning of their own awakening to a more mature faith.

Discerning the Gospel

Our approach depends on a correlation of the gospel with human need. The guide must discern the gospel for the situation. What is the appropriate truth to emphasize in this instance?

To offer a complete guide to the discernment of the gospel for human need would be synonymous with an exposition of the entire New Testament. Obviously such an endeavor would be more confusing than enlightening. On the other hand, our purpose could be aided by describing one form of discerning the gospel, an illustration of which would enable the guide to explore other options.

The metaphors Christ used to describe himself provide a model for discerning the gospel. If every person engages in a search for meaning, if the search for meaning is a disguised search for the will of God, and if Christ is the will of God made flesh, then the metaphors Christ applied to himself reveal both the will of God and the fulfillment of our lives.

Think about the metaphors of bread, of a door, and of life as symbols of the soul's deepest longings. These symbols, which speak explicitly of human need, also point to Christ. These symbols have the power to mediate the presence of Christ as a solution to human need. All persons hunger for meaning in their lives. Christ portrays himself as "the bread of life," so the metaphor of bread correlates with the experience of hunger.

In this model, the guide discerns the person and then discerns which gospel metaphor most appropriately speaks to the particular situation. This model presupposes that Christ is the answer to the human dilemma and that the metaphors reflect different aspects of the answer. With this matrix in mind, we will explore the metaphors of Christ in the Gospel of John and apply them to various existential situations.

Bread

Jesus said, "I am the bread of life; he who comes to me shall not hunger, and he who believes in me shall never thirst" (John 6:35). Christ as the bread of life feeds the soul as bread feeds the body. This metaphor points to the nature of God as the one who nurtures and sustains us. To eat of this bread brings deep satisfaction to the soul. I know a young man who had been doing drugs and drinking heavily for several years. One Sunday morning, for reasons he could not articulate, he decided against going with friends for a beer bash in the mountains. Alone at home, he turned on the television. On the screen a man held the Bible in his left hand as he spoke about Christ as "the bread of life." The symbol of bread awakened my friend to faith. In the days that followed, he received strength to do God's will.

Does the couple's desire to have their baby baptized indicate a hunger?

Light

Jesus said, "I am the light of the world; he who follows me will not walk in darkness, but will have the light of life" (John 8:12). Light derives from the sun, which enables a person to see. Light by derivation illuminates the mind to understand what is seen. Christ as light enables persons to understand the meaning of their lives and illumines the direction for them to take. In the instance just mentioned, the young man could see no purpose for his life until his mind was enlightened by Christ. While the light did not completely reveal the future, Christ *did* give him an immediate conviction that his life had meaning. His darkness and uncertainty were penetrated by the light of Christ. As he began to walk in the light given him, additional light came at various times and places on his journey.

By requesting baptism for their son, is the couple seeking light?

Door

Jesus said, "Truly, truly I say to you, I am the door of the sheep" (John 10:7). The door permits the sheep to enter into the fold. If they do not find the door, they wander outside, exposed to the wolves, and live at great risk. The door admits them to the fold, where they will be safe. In the fold the shepherd feeds and cares for them. A door opens new possibilities for life. A door opens new directions for the future; it also closes out the past. The door opens the way into life.

A man in his mid-twenties came into my study before the service. "I'm desperate," he said. "My wife has been having an affair with our neighbor. She has now left me and taken our daughter. What am I going to do?"

In his desperation this man was seeking a door. From his perspective, life looked impossible. He saw no way into the future.

Can I not say to him, "I sense your desperation. You have no place to go. Christ is a doorway into new possibilities for you."

Are Matthew's parents reaching for a doorway into new life?

Shepherd

Jesus said, "I am the good shepherd. The good shepherd lays down his life for the sheep" (John 10:11). As a shepherd he knows the sheep by name, leads them, cares for them. The central emphasis of the shepherd metaphor falls upon tenderness, caring, and knowing the sheep intimately.

Who needs a shepherd? Is it not those who feel uncared for, who have been marginalized by society? A woman came to be baptized. She had already made her profession of faith. In preparation for the sacrament, I spoke with her about the church and what it meant to be baptized. Her clothes and her demeanor suggested that she did not share the cultural background of most of the membership.

After several minutes of conversation in preparation for baptism, I asked her the question, "Will you be loyal to Christ and his people and will you accept all who worship with us?"

Quick as a flash, she said, "Preacher, you better say that to the rest of the members, because they haven't done much to welcome me!"

One does not need penetrating discernment to hear her hunger for a caring shepherd.

Apply the metaphor to the couple seeking baptism for their son. Are they in need of a shepherd?

Vine

Again, Jesus said, "I am the vine, you are the branches. He who abides in me, and I in him, he it is that bears much fruit, for apart from me you can do nothing" (John 15:5). The vine provides the source of life. If a branch does not bear much fruit, the gardener prunes it; if it bears no fruit, he cuts it off and throws it into the fire.

Is not this metaphor for those whose life has become dry and fruitless? Perhaps once they had faith. Through neglect they have lost touch with Christ. Their life shows the loss.

I met Jackie after her return to the church. It had been a long and painful road back. In her mid-twenties, Christ had been very near, but she lost her support system when she had to move, and her life had gone on the skids. After telling me her story, she wanted to know if she could ever feel connected again.

Her hunger suggests the vine metaphor. Through neglect and disillusionment, she had turned from her early faith. Yet the emptiness of her life and the memory of better times compelled her to look for the connection again.

Are the parents in our interview in need of pruning? Have they become fruitless?

The Way

The last of the metaphors I will explore gathers up all the others—the way, the truth, and the life. Jesus said, "I am the way, and the truth, and the life. No one comes to the Father, but by me" (John 14:6). The way to God is through Christ; the way to live has been shown us in Christ.

In an age of pluralism, in which persons say, "There are many ways to God," the Christian guide must hold up the metaphor of the way. When persons deny all absolutes, the Christian must hold to the absoluteness of Jesus Christ as "the way, the truth, and the life."

I have struggled with this issue for a long time; I have spoken about it with colleagues. We must claim his absoluteness as the way to God; we must make this witness in humility, respect, and love. But we must make it!

Which of these metaphors could the minister have used in discernment of the gospel? Was this couple manifesting a hunger? Were they seeking new possibilities or a new direction? Do they show a need for warmth and tenderness? In a modest way are they seeking to reconnect?

Does not the metaphor of "the way, the truth, and the life" speak to their situation? They have been away from the church; a child has been born in their home; they are beginning again.

Perhaps the metaphor of "the vine" also speaks to them. They have been barren for these past few years; they have felt cut off from the source of life. Does not this time of baptism offer them an opportunity to be engrafted onto the vine?

The Transition

When we hold up the metaphors of Christ to the needs of persons, they do not always make an immediate transition. They may not "see the light," or enter the "door," or eat the "bread of life." Jesus' own tactics may prove helpful to the guide in these transitional experiences. Recall some of the ways he directed persons who did not at first respond to him.

Jesus invited persons to investigate. When the disciples of John followed Jesus they asked, "Rabbi, where are you staying?"

He said to them, "Come and see" (John 1:39).

The guide may invite this couple to look more deeply into the truth of Christ, to ask questions that arise from their experience. The faith of Christ will stand up under analysis.

Christ used affirmation. Recall the woman who had been apprehended committing adultery. After her accusers filed out of the meeting, Jesus spoke to the woman. "Where are your accusers? Does no one condemn you?"

She said, "No one, sir!"

Jesus said, "Neither do I condemn you; go, and sin no more" (see John 8:10–11).

This encounter demonstrates that "God sent the Son into the world, not to condemn the world, but that the world might be saved through him" (John 3:17).

Does not this couple need affirmation? They have gone away from the church, but God still loves them. Are they not indicating a concern by their desire for their son's baptism?

Jesus always dealt lovingly with persons. Paul may have been thinking about Christ when he wrote, "Love is patient and kind; love is not jealous or boastful; it is not arrogant or rude. Love does not insist on its own way; it is not irritable or resentful. . . . Love bears all things, believes all things, hopes all things, endures all things" (1 Cor. 13:4–5,7).

Guides must always deal with persons with love. In spite of our anxiety, we must care for persons. In the case of the family we have described, they certainly need love more than condemnation.

Jesus prepared persons. Recall Jesus' visit to Jerusalem for the Passover, when many believed in him because of the signs (John 2:23). But Jesus did not entrust himself to the multitude. He knew what was in their hearts, and he realized they were not ready to receive him.

Our work in spiritual guidance endeavors to prepare persons to make a response to Christ. Christ does not commit himself to unprepared hearts.

Frank could have been more effective in preparing Ralph and Linda. If he had listened to their stories, they would have gotten in touch with memories of God's nearness to them.

Ralph and Linda Revisited

The analysis of Frank's visit with Ralph and Linda is not meant as a criticism of this sincere minister. He sought earnestly to accomplish his task. He admitted that he did not have positive feelings about the visit. With keener discernment how could he have been more helpful in guiding Ralph and Linda toward a renewed faith?

I believe a few changes in Frank's approach would have made a considerable difference. Walking through the visit again and noting a few changes may help with our discernment of the persons and the gospel.

Frank began by creating an atmosphere of warmth and genuine interest in Ralph and Linda. The environment for discernment certainly should be relaxed and nonthreatening.

Instead of beginning with the "why" question, "Why do you want to have Matthew baptized?" perhaps he would have served his purpose better by saying, "I've had very little opportunity to get to know you since your return to the States. What can you tell me about yourself?" An open-ended question would have given Ralph and Linda freedom to choose the subject for discussion. I suspect he would have heard about their early life in the church, their college days, marriage, and the trek overseas. What they said and how they said it would have given Frank a "feel" for the couple before getting into the issues surrounding baptism.

Frank might have introduced the baptism by saying, "I know that both of you were reared in the church, and you probably were baptized as children. Have you ever heard the story of your baptism? I would like to hear the stories you have been told about that day, if you recall them." This suggestion invites them to recall part of their own history; in recalling, they will reconnect with the event. Let us imagine that one of them told a story of baptism. After hearing the story, Frank might have said, "Sunday we will be creating that kind of story for you to tell Matthew when he grows up." A connection of their story with Matthew would have eased the atmosphere and would probably have elicited positive feelings.

Since baptism marks our entrance into the church, Frank could have talked with the parents about the meaning of Christian initiation. Since both of them had been baptized and are members of the church, he could have said, "I would like to hear what being part of the church has meant in your lives." This gives Ralph and Linda an opportunity to review their connection with the church. We know that they were reared in the church, moved away during their college years, and are now making their way back to the church. Recounting this journey would touch deep feelings, the kind of feelings that motivated them to have Matthew baptized. All these stories would have given Frank better information for his discernment.

Listening to their stories would also have created a warmer environment. The initial question—"Why do you wish to have Matthew baptized?"—could have been softened. Frank might have said, "From your own experience you know the value of baptism and the church. How would you put into words your desire for Matthew?"

After listening to the stories that these questions would evoke, Frank would have had a deeper relation with Ralph and Linda. They would have been engaged through the conversation, they would have reviewed their lives, and they would be better prepared to deal with the vows for the baptism. Frank might have introduced the first question by saying, "Sunday, I will ask each of you to state your faith in Jesus Christ. You made this confession when you joined the church, and this offers you an opportunity to renew it. Can you think of one thing this renewal might mean to you?"

Frank's handling of the "covenant promises" seemed pretty awkward. Maybe if he had explained that "God has promised to accept us in Jesus Christ, and when you bring Matthew this Sunday, you are saying, 'Lord, we claim your promise to accept Matthew.' So when you come forward and stand before the congregation, think of yourself and the congregation as claiming God's promise for Matthew."

He could continue, "I will also ask you to promise to be an example for Matthew. Can you think of some practices that would be a good example?" From the original interview we know they are aware of faith, prayer, and forgiveness. The minister could also add practices they may have forgotten.

After this conversation it would be quite natural for Frank to invite this couple to renew their dedication to Christ as they present Matthew for baptism. Frank might have said, "I appreciate the way you have shared your lives with me tonight. As a representative of Christ, I invite you to renew your own commitment as you present Matthew for Christian baptism."

From what we know about Ralph and Linda, we conclude that they need a new beginning in obedience to Christ. Frank has an opportunity to extend the invitation. He need not press the point, but he should articulate it. Would not hearing the invitation be of significance to them?

Before leaving, Frank should have a brief prayer with the parents that God will enable them to do what they are promising in the vows of baptism.

What specific changes does this approach make? Does it provide a better basis for discernment?

The Invitation to Faith

In each encounter with another, the spiritual guide seeks to take the action that will help the subject respond to Christ. This point of contact, called many different things, brings a new center of awareness of Christ. The effective guide will always keep this concern central.

John Westerhoff identifies four elements as necessary for an authentic conversion: (1) a knowledge of alternatives (the guide must realize that secularism, Eastern religion, or hedonism, as well as Christian faith, are options); (2) personal struggle (to engage in an assessment of other forms of faith in comparison with Christ); (3) nurture (study, conversations with believers, and worship); and (4) a free decision (space to make one's own choice without feeling pressured or manipulated). These demands inform the guide's role.[1]

The guide always operates in the tension between faithfulness to Christ and respect for the subject, between human action and divine action. No rules can be constructed, but the safest guidance is love for Christ and love for the person.

In initial guidance, one key role of the guide will be issuing invitations. Most often the sensitive guide issues small, gentle invitations rather than hard, confrontative ones, though sometimes more direct invitations are in order. Gentle invitations may be: "Have you considered . . . ? May I suggest . . . ? Would you be willing . . . ?" A hard invitation: "Will you give yourself to Christ today? Will you here and now accept his promise?"

Extending the invitation is the easiest aspect of guidance to neglect. Yet the invitation is, in many ways, the most crucial aspect of the work of a spiritual guide. When and how does the guide extend the invitation to faith? Gentle invitations may be extended naturally in a variety of conversations, but direct invitations require proper timing.

Thomas Green suggests three elements that are essential if a guide is to be effective in discernment. These qualities also apply to the guide's extending the invitation to begin the journey of faith. First, the guide must have a desire to do God's will. In encounters with persons, a guide must desire God's will above all else. At times this will require the guide to lay aside timidity or fear of rejection when the invitation is extended. Second, the guide must have an openness to God. To be open means that the guide may experience God in mysterious, surprising, and disturbing ways. In this arena of faith responses, the guide must not be put off by unexpected questions and reactions. Third, the guide must have a knowledge of God.[2] This knowledge of God is acquired through experience. How can guides discern what God wills if they do not know God?

8

Making the Connection

Discerning the need and discerning the gospel prepare an individual to respond, to take the leap of faith, to trust putting oneself into the hands of God. What is the guide's role in facilitating this encounter?

Initial spiritual direction, which we are calling evangelism, seeks to connect a person with God. Just as the electric lamp lacks power before it is plugged into the socket, an individual lacks the energy of Christ until that person has made conscious contact with God. In chapter 3 we explored the triadic nature of the God/guide/subject. Now we inquire more deeply into the question of how the guide helps the subject to enter into a conscious relationship with God. A concrete situation will provide a context for our discussion.

Diane made an attempt to help Janice come to a personal consciousness of Christ in her life. Janice was divorced, a parent in her early forties. For the past few months she had been attending Sunday school at Diane's church, but she never participated in worship.

Diane encountered her at the supermarket and opened a conversation by asking, "What do you think of our church?"

"I don't like the worship service," Janice responded. "I can't relate to what the minister says. His talk about Jesus as our Savior turns me off."

"I notice you bring a Bible to church. Do you study it?" inquired Diane.

"I go to Sunday school—the people in that class stood by me when I was going through my divorce. I still feel their support." With that affirmation she came to the question Diane had asked about Bible study. "For a while I studied with the Jehovah's Witnesses; I thought they could give me some answers, but there are just too many contradictions."

Sensing her willingness to talk about scripture, Diane asked, "What are you studying now?"

"Revelation," she said, with a smile and a raised eyebrow. "You know, I'd like to ask you a question. It says in Revelation that those persons whose names are not written in the book of life will be thrown into a lake of fire. I don't worry about going to hell, but burning in a lake of fire really bothers me. Is that going to happen to me?"

"Are you afraid God is going to punish you?" Diane asked.

"The Jehovah's Witnesses taught me that when you are dead, you are dead, but this verse says more than that."

"Janice, I'm going to be honest with you. I can't tell you whether you will burn in a lake of fire, but what you have said raises an important question in my mind."

"What's that?"

"What is your image of God? What's God like to you?"

"God is someone I can plug into when things go wrong. I get a lot of comfort out of knowing God is with me in crises like my divorce, or the problems I've had with my children, or my mother's illness."

"I see."

"But," continued Diane, "when everything is okay, I get back into my regular life until I need God again."

"What do you think would happen if you plugged into God all the time?"

This important question provides a background against which to define the elements in human agency in the evangelizing process. Realizing that Diane cannot give Janice faith, but also recognizing that she has both a desire and an obligation to assist Janice, what can one person do to help another come to a personal faith? How is the connection with God made?

Four Approaches

In Diane's effort to be of help to Janice and be faithful to her calling to share her faith, four possible avenues were open to her—rational, emotional, moral, and imaginative ones. Diane could have picked up on Janice's doctrinal problem and quoted scripture affirming the uniqueness and absoluteness of Christ. In addition she could have presented to her the plan of salvation, much like the approach described in chapter 4. These responses would have been a straightforward, rational approach.

Diane could have chosen an emotional approach. Janice states that she did not believe in hell but had concerns about burning in a lake of fire. Diane could have seized upon her anxiety, presented the gospel plan to her, and invited her to believe in Christ as an escape from the lake of fire. Or she could have switched from fear to self-interest and offered Janice a Christ who would bring assurance, comfort, and happiness. In the first case the witness appeals to fear and offers an escape from punishment; in the second, the witness promises a reward for believing. Both of these would be emotional responses.

A third option would have been to suggest new forms of behavior. The suggestions might have been, "You have found God to be faithful when you call out for help; what you should do now is attend church regularly, bring your children to church, study your Bible more diligently, and live the kind of life you know you should." This suggestion leads directly to a "works righteousness," saved by doing what we know is right—a moralistic approach to salvation.

But, interestingly, Diane chose none of these approaches to help Janice get related to God. She chose the way of imagination: "What do you think would happen if you should plug into God all the time?" With this perceptive question, Diane invited Janice to imagine a new relationship with God that issued in a new way of being and living.

Conversion always involves an imaginative shift in perception. In the moment of conversion, persons begin to perceive reality in a new way; the data of their lives may remain essentially the same, but they are seen in a new light. The new way of seeing transforms everything for the individual. A colleague once asked what I thought conversion meant. I said, "Conversion means a transformation of one's worldview—the way we see God, the world, ourselves, and our relation to God."

This shift of perception finds confirmation in scripture. Consider the experience of the fishermen and Jesus. One day as John was baptizing, he pointed to a stranger who was approaching, saying, "Behold, the Lamb of God who takes away the sin of the world!" (John 1:29). Andrew heard the affirmation and followed Jesus home. After spending several hours with him, Andrew found Simon Peter and announced to him that Jesus was the Christ. Sometime later Jesus said to both Peter and Andrew, "Come, follow me and I will make you fishers of men" (see Mark 1:17). In the intervening weeks Jesus had not changed and Andrew's and Peter's lives had not changed; they were still fishermen. But they had begun to imagine new possibilities for their lives and thus were able to respond to his invitation to become a follower. In the process they had been unaware of him, noted him as a stranger, heard him proclaimed Messiah, and then received a personal invitation to follow. At each of these stages they experienced a change in their imaginative perception.

Paul also provides a clear illustration of "seeing." When he left Jerusalem on a mission to Damascus to apprehend and jail all the Christians, he saw himself as faithful to God, an enemy of Jesus of Nazareth, and obedient to the faith. But on the way he encountered Christ. The encounter with Christ spontaneously changed his perception of God, himself, and the believers in Damascus (see Acts 9:1–19). Conversion meant a new way of seeing and a new way of being in the world. So the man who set out to Damascus to persecute Christians had, in fact, become one by the time he arrived.

When, therefore, we seek to help persons come to personal faith in Christ, we are inviting them to "see" in a different way. With the invitation to imagine, we have gone to the limit of human capability, but at that point the Holy Spirit energizes the imagination to "see" and through that spiritual impulse conversion occurs. This transformation does not depend on human logic, the power of persuasion, or manipulation of any kind, but on the Spirit. And when the Spirit acts upon the imagination to change another, that event transforms the person's reason, emotions, and will—the whole person.

Imagination and Conversion

I have been helped in my thinking about the role of the imagination in conversion by the work of Garrett Green.[1] Green argues that the revelation of God—or conversion, as we describe it—occurs in the imagination by a sudden paradigm shift; we view life in one frame of reference and suddenly we see it in another. Green builds his case on insights gained from Kuhn's *Structure of Scientific Revolutions.*[2] Kuhn asserts that in traditional science a theory grows piecemeal: it is a "cumulative process, gathering facts by empirical observation, then formulating, testing, and revising theories against established facts and new observations."[3] This is the scientific method.

Changes, or scientific revolutions, occur when existing paradigms become problematic. For example, a scientific theory like Ptolemy's view of the earth as the center of the universe, with the sun rotating around it, was weakened when the data supporting the original theory were challenged by overwhelming contradictory evidence. The more the contradictory data increase, the greater the tension on the original theory; this tension grows to the breaking point and the scientist's confidence in the old theory breaks down, causing the shift to another theory. Kuhn advises that the "decision to reject one paradigm is always simultaneously the decision to accept another."[4] The scientist, like the unbeliever, cannot stand in a no-man's-land.

The shift to a new paradigm is abrupt; it is never evolutionary. Kuhn argues that established views are "interpreted and transformed by 'scientific revolutions' that change the rules, the methods and instrumentation, and even the meaning of the basic concepts used in scientific thinking."[5]

Interestingly, Kuhn calls these paradigm shifts in scientific thought a "conversion."[6] The scientist who makes this shift at an early stage does so with real risk; he has faith that the new way will succeed. Kuhn says the decision for a new paradigm is one that "can only be made on faith."[7]

A pause to suggest what this analysis of a scientific paradigm shift adds to our search will help. Kuhn has shown how scientific paradigms grow through a theory that accumulates data piecemeal. In many respects this is precisely how one's life story and one's view of the world develop. In the community of origin, the meaning of life for us is formed by the pictures of the world, the models of humanness, and the rules by which life is to be lived. These data and images come unbidden, and we absorb them unconsciously. In this manner we develop our view of the world and the place we have in it. Unreflectively we assimilate new data of all sorts into the dominant paradigm. In contrast to the scientist consciously forming a hypothesis, our process of "world building" is quite unconscious.

This view of reality absorbed unconsciously serves well enough until experiences in life create tension with it. Tension may be produced by an unexplained loss, a serious illness, a hunger for deeper meaning, or, perhaps, a revelatory experience of God. This tension also occurs when we marry and discover our spouse perceives reality differently; it happens when young people go away to college and meet a new world. Certain contradictory experiences begin to create doubt about the old paradigm, the old way of being and seeing. When that tension becomes great enough, persons are motivated to change. But, as in a scientific paradigm shift, the person will not forsake the old way of viewing the world until a new way has been acquired. Christian faith, the Christian vision of reality, provides this new way of looking to which a person with an inadequate vision may turn.

As it is for the scientist, the shift from the old to the new way of "seeing" appears to be a jump more than an evolution. It requires faith and is taken with a degree of risk.

With this correlation of conversion with a scientific paradigm shift, we can continue to explore with Garrett Green the manner of the paradigm shift. By paradigm we mean a pattern or model. Kuhn uses paradigm to refer to an essential pattern for viewing nature or a part of nature. The paradigm becomes the key to the terminology and methodology of a particular approach.

To this definition of a paradigm, Green adds a valuable insight from the Gestalt psychologists, who claim that "our perception of 'parts' depends on our prior grasp of a 'whole.' "[8] This principle of a holistic functioning of our perception can be illustrated by certain optical illusions. Take the well-known picture of the old witch/young woman (see Figure 5). Some persons perceive the old woman first, others the young one. Why?

FIGURE 5.

Or, consider Figure 6. What do you see? Is it a duck or a rabbit? According to the Gestalt psychologists, a particular structure of the psyche causes us to see one or the other of these objects first. We do not look at certain lines but at the whole of the representation; the way we see the whole determines how we see the parts. According to Green, a paradigm functions like a gestalt—they are models that we use to grasp the whole of reality. A change in paradigm changes one's view of the world. Green says, "Those 'changes of world-view,' like the paradigms on which they are based, are discontinuous, incommensurable, irreversible, and highly resistant to verification or falsification."[9]

FIGURE 6.

What does this paradigm shift mean in a concrete situation—Janice's, for example? From what we know about Janice, she seeks God primarily in emergencies. Some vision other than the gospel, like fate or chance, seems to be the dominant paradigm. Diane invited her to consider a vision of reality that placed God at the center of life and deeply involved with all of life. Diane's invitation challenged her to look at God in a different way.

The paradigm shift can also be illustrated in the perceptual change from law to grace. If a woman has been reared to believe that she must earn approval, life will be seen as a testing ground for earning the desired reward. When she fails to measure up to the rules, her self-worth, her feeling of competency, and her role in life will come into question.

Suppose this same woman encounters the gospel. In the life, death, and resurrection of Christ she sees an alternative world, one of grace and not law. In an imaginative leap she trusts in a God who loves the unlovely and forgives sinful people. This leap involves a paradigm shift, a different way of "seeing." This shift gives her new eyes, and she views reality from a new perspective, a gestalt of grace; her failures have been forgiven, her self-worth restored, and her life given a purpose. The new vision of reality permits her to perceive and interpret her life in a completely new and different manner.

For our purpose of helping persons come to faith in Christ in a way that changes them, we must, according to Green, offer them a model of reality, a worldview that the gospel calls into being. When the contradictions in their present model become sharp enough, they may embrace this "reality vision," which answers the deeper needs of their lives.

But how does this shift occur? Where does it take place? Green suggests that this shift in our way of seeing occurs in the imagination. He defines imagination as "an image or picture representing some object that is not directly accessible to the imagining subject."[10] Before describing the creative use of the imagination, it is probably best to acknowledge that the imagination can operate in both a positive and negative fashion. It can function in both real and illusory ways. For example, we mean very different things when we say that one person has "imaginative leadership" and another one imagines ghosts in the attic.

This powerful capacity to imagine can readily be seen in the use of memory. To recall an experience from the past is an act of placing images of past experience into our mind in the present. Memory gives us an opportunity to make new decisions about the occurrences represented by the images, and it also makes possible our picturing a new and different future. Augustine's *Confessions* offers one example of a man reliving his whole life through memory and reintegrating his past in terms of the new future created by faith in Christ.

But imagination is not confined to recalling images from the past; it also functions in the present as we interpret the occurrences in our lives. For example, one day a man goes to work feeling his future is secure, but when he arrives he is fired. To achieve a degree of stability he must interpret this event. The manner in which he "sees" the world will inform his imaginative interpretation of this shocking blow. If he has embraced a fatalistic view of the world, his job loss will be an impersonal stroke of fate. On the other hand, if he views the world as directed by God, he will trust that God has some purpose in what seems to be a tragedy. The interpretation of what happens in our lives occurs through an established paradigm, the way we "see" it.

Green suggests one more potent aspect of this interpretative imagination. "The realistic imagination thus depends entirely on paradigms to gain access to the 'transcendent,' taken here in the literal sense as the 'world beyond.' "[11] Viewing the imagination as the domain in which we human beings experience the transcendent does not mean that the imagination has the inherent power to grasp the divine. Rather, it implies that when this function is moved upon by the Holy Spirit, revelation occurs. The revelation of God occurs in the imagination. The paradigmatic imagination under the impact of the Spirit creates a new world. In our opening narrative we saw Diane invite Janice to imagine a different relation with God: "What do you think would happen if you plugged into God all the time?" To imagine this new experience of God, Janice needs more and better information. As she learns that God is with her, that God loves her, and that God wills good things for her life, these perceptions acted upon by the Spirit will create new and alternative images of her future.

If the imagination depends on paradigms to grasp the transcendent, what happens when a person's paradigm is negative like Janice's? Or what if the paradigm is opaque? Suppose persons have been reared in a culture in which God has no part. The paradigm by which they perceive and interpret life lacks the capacity to open human experience to the beyond, the transcendent. The inadequate paradigm confines these persons to a two-dimensional work—length and breadth but no depth.

I believe Green offers further insight into this capacity when he suggests, "The paradigmatic imagination is the ability to see one thing as another."[12] In the duck/rabbit illustration the lines on the page do not change, but the shift in perception changes what is seen by the viewer's eye. In a similar manner when one's life history is viewed through the holistic lenses of the Christian paradigm, the events composing that history do not change; they lie quiet and still in the past. But in conversion the paradigmatic imagination perceives those events through the grace of God, and their significance changes radically.

Since this view of the role of imagination in conversion may be new for many of us, perhaps it will be of value to summarize our findings. What do paradigms, gestalts, and imagination have to do with conversion? How do they inform the task of helping a person come to faith in Christ?

If Green's line of reasoning is correct, we may assume that all persons possess a paradigm through which they view the world. For our purposes, how they perceive the God/human, God/world relation holds primary importance. "Conversion" refers to the dramatic shift in perception from a self-centered to a God-centered vision of the world. This shift not only affects "seeing" but feeling, behaving, and valuing—a holistic shift. To be of assistance to others, the guide must recognize their particular paradigm. The guide can offer biblical and personal images, pictures, and narratives that nurture the imagination and thereby participate with the Spirit in feeding the paradigmatic imagination.

A Model of Connecting

After this excursion into the role of the imagination in conversion we will pick up where we left off with Janice. Diane shared her faith with Janice, then urged her to give the minister another chance—maybe attendance at church or a conversation on a person-to-person basis. One Sunday morning Janice reluctantly attended worship again, and this time the sermon seemed different. Over the next few months she worshiped with a fair degree of regularity and one Sunday on her way out the door said to the minister, "I would like to talk with you sometime." To her surprise, he reached under his robe, pulled out his appointment book, and set a time that week to see her.

The date for the appointment came. The minister opened the conversation with a statement of his desire to know Janice. The minister's interest in making an appointment with her had already begun to change her feelings, so she felt more open to tell him about herself. She began by sharing with him her positive experience in the Sunday school. Reluctantly, she described her search in Bible study groups with the Jehovah's Witnesses and her fear about burning in a lake of fire. She repeated to the minister her conversation with Diane and Diane's certainty about her faith.

When the minister asked her about her image of God, she told him she had received comfort in times of crisis but that afterward she got back into her regular life. When the minister sought to explore more carefully her notion of God, he found it to be rather vague. At this point the minister helped Janice get a more accurate perception of the Christian faith before inviting a decision.

Janice's issues were the person of Jesus, a God who helps through crises, and fear of the lake of fire. The minister told Janice to place her emphasis on God's will for her, rather than on escaping the lake of fire. She also needed a picture of God that included more than filling the gaps in times of crisis, and she required a clearer picture of Christ.

"I recognize your fear of burning in a lake of fire," the minister told her. "If that were to happen, it would be a very fearful thing for anyone. Let me assure you that God does not desire that for you or for anyone else—God loves you!"

This affirmation began to allay Janice's fear and to open to her a positive view of God. To further assist Janice in her image of God, the minister rehearsed the story of creation, a God who desired to share the divine presence with creatures made in the divine image. The rehearsal, which began with creation, concluded with Jesus, who came to show us God and bring us back to God—the picture we have set forth in the triadic structure. This narrative presentation gave her another paradigm through which to view her life. Do we not see how a faulty paradigm blocks or distorts the imagination? Providing gospel images serves to correct these problems.

If Janice had asked about the person of Jesus Christ, an issue that arose from her contact with Jehovah's Witnesses, she would not need a lecture on Christology but a simple witness that Christ makes God known to us.

Suppose that the minister's explanations offered relief to Janice; she still had more investigating to do, but after the appointment she was open to consider the Christian faith. How does the minister nurture her paradigmatic imagination? Four ways are open to him: gospel narrative, personal narrative, memory, and a direct appeal to her imagination. The minister could suggest to Janice that she reminded him of a woman who came to Jesus feeling quite desperate about her life.

"May I read her story to you?"

With permission granted, he would open the Bible and read from Mark 5, verses 24 to 34:

> And a great crowd followed him and thronged about him. And there was a woman who had had a flow of blood for twelve years, and who had suffered much under many physicians, and had spent all that she had, and was no better but rather grew worse. She had heard the reports about Jesus, and came up behind him in the crowd and touched his garment. For she said, "If I touch even his garments, I shall be made well." And immediately the hemorrhage ceased; and she felt in her body that she was healed of her disease. And Jesus, perceiving in himself that power had gone forth from him, immediately turned about in the crowd, and said, "Who touched my garments?" And his disciples said to him, "You see the crowd pressing around you, and yet you say, 'Who touched me?' " And he looked around to see who had done it. But the woman, knowing what had been done to her, came in fear and trembling and fell down before him, and told him the whole truth. And he said to her, "Daughter, your faith has made you well; go in peace, and be healed of your disease."

After reading the scripture, the minister could have asked Janice, "Do you see any of yourself in this woman? Would you consider the possibility that your faith might do the same thing for you? What would it mean for you to touch Jesus' garment today?"

If Janice still faces troublesome questions about Jesus, the minister must deal with them; they cannot be glossed over. This may not be the day she can make a connection with God through Christ. In reading this story and by inviting Janice to become part of the story, the minister uses biblical images to offer her a new paradigm through which to view her life. The questions are intended to stimulate her imagination.

Another approach to Janice's imagination could be through her memory. She has revealed two aspects of her life to which the minister may refer—the Sunday school class and the times God has helped her. The minister may ask her to tell about one of those times. With the request Janice begins to think back and says, "When my mother was ill, I was so afraid. I recall praying to God for help. After about three days I began to feel at peace, and in my heart I knew that Mom would be all right."

"Could you say something else about how you prayed? In what way did God give you peace? How did your thoughts change? Is not this God interested in you all the time and not just in the crises of your life?"

These questions would perhaps have been helpful to Janice in making a life-changing connection with God. All of them invite her to an expanded awareness of God. Do not these images "seed" her consciousness with positive pictures of God?

Diane has given her witness to Janice, who remembers her statements. The minister also has his own testimony. Suppose he recalls to Janice, "When God became real in my life, I did not know anything much about Jesus Christ. I had been to Sunday school; I learned the song 'Jesus Loves Me, This I Know,' but I knew nothing of the doctrines of the Christian faith. With something of a risk, I placed my faith in God, a God who loved me." These questions might follow the minister's witness:

"I wonder if you have ever entrusted your life to God? What would it mean to you to make this decision? How could I be of help to you in making this choice?"

In addition to scripture, personal memory, and Christian testimony, the minister may appeal directly to Janice's imagination:

"Janice, what if God loves you more than anyone else

in the world can love you? What if God has been with you through thick and thin and you have not recognized this divine presence? What if God only wants you to say 'yes' to God's call to you? What if God desires to be with you in every experience of your life, to guide you and care for you?"

These questions invite Janice to view her life through a different paradigm. Perhaps new visions provide the prelude to conversion, but efforts to manipulate the imagination should be steadily rejected. Redemptive work in the imagination must be inspired by the Spirit; anything else produces illusion.

A few months passed. Janice continued to worship and showed signs of a deepening interest. One day she phoned and said, "Pastor, I need to talk with you."

Before she came for the appointment, the minister knew that he could not deliver God to her. God is sovereign and therefore free. But this minister was called and sent by God to persons like Janice who need God. His efforts at helping her take place in the space between God's sovereignty and Janice's freedom and dignity.

After five minutes of conversation, Janice asked, "Pastor, tell me: How do I get God in my life?"

The minister had several pieces of information at his disposal: she had had a painful divorce; she received support from a Sunday school class; she had heard a member's testimony; she had begun attending worship; she had expressed her doubts about Jesus and her fear about burning in a lake of fire; now, she was asking a straightforward question: "How do I get God in my life?"

The minister could give her the plan of salvation, offer prayer, and in faith claim God in her life. While this response might make a turning point for her, it seemed to be jumping into the water before she knew the pool's depth. So the minister said, "Explain, please, what you mean when you say you want to get God in your life."

Janice began to draw circles around her intended meaning with a few anecdotal statements. "I heard you say that God is the answer to an empty life and that persons will never experience real life until they know God on a daily basis."

The minister nodded as she spoke.

"And," she said, "Diane, who spoke to me a few months ago, has continued to phone me, speak to me at church, and share her faith with me. She seems to have such joy in her life!"

Janice said that her life had been empty. Worship had awakened an interest, and she experienced Christian caring from Diane. These influences plus her Sunday school experience combined to deepen her awareness. "To get God in her life" seemed to mean inner peace and a changed life. (This was not the moment to talk with Janice about "consumer religion," "cheap grace," or "positive thinking religion." She had been awakened to her need for faith and she revealed a genuine openness to make a change.)

At this point, it occurred to the minister that he might need to reinforce Janice's Christian frame of reference to help her respond to this stirring in her soul. "Janice," he began, "may I share with you some information that I think will help answer your question about getting God in your life?" (Notice he used her language to talk with her about God.)

"Sure, go ahead!"

"This matter of getting God into our lives has deep roots in the human story." He described the entrance of sin into human experience and the negative consequences it had upon our consciousness of God. Then he explained that God loved us and came to us in Christ. In Christ, God opened the way for us to be related to God in acceptance. He told Janice that the Spirit of God had been poured out in the world and is active in all persons, but most don't notice the Spirit.

When he paused, Janice asked, "Do you suppose the Spirit you speak of was the source of that comfort I felt from God in my times of crisis?"

In this response, Janice made an imaginative leap from the truth of the gospel to her own experience. This appeared to be a revelatory moment for her.

"But how do I have God as a part of my whole life and not just as an occasional visitor?" she asked.

"When you entrust your life to Christ though faith, God comes into your life; God creates a new center of consciousness within you." (It didn't seem necessary to tell Janice this was a new birth, a justification by faith. That explanation could come later.)

"Can you now entrust yourself to Christ?" the minister asked. "He will enter your life as a resident."

"I want to very much," she responded, "but I'm scared."

"With the gentleness of a mother, God has come to you, sending caring persons into your life, offering you a new beginning, and putting enough faith in you to ask, 'How can I get God in my life?' I believe God is inviting you into a permanent conscious relationship."

Janice paused a moment. "I too believe that God has been doing something in my life, and I want to say yes."

With his accumulated wisdom, the minister said, "Let's sit here quietly before the Lord. In the silence you tell God that you are giving as much of yourself as you can to as much of God as you understand."

After a few moments the minister said, "Thanks be to you, O God, for coming to Janice, for claiming her today as your child. Help her to grow in faith and in love for you. Amen."

The next Sunday the pastor surveyed the congregation, and his eyes met Janice's. He knew she had been grasped by God's love. Every inch of her face reflected the reality of the divine presence. In a flash it occurred to him: "Helping persons know God—this is what ministry is all about."

9

Person, Process, and Pitfalls

Spiritual guidance may begin at one of two places in making another person aware of God. In the following example, Charlie Roberts, the minister, could have begun with the gospel or with the person's life experience.

Charlie had been at the church less than a year. One morning a new member telephoned to ask him to visit her nephew, Jim Allgood, who she felt was experiencing stress from his work and his marriage. The minister agreed to go to Jim's office later in the day.

"Good afternoon, Mr. Allgood," the minister said. "I'm glad that I could come by. Your aunt said you would be expecting me."

Jim responded with a warm welcome. "I'm glad you could come by today."

"Well, Jim, how are things going?"

With a sigh and a wrinkled brow Jim said, "I really don't know where to begin. There are so many things I'm dealing with, I don't know which one to tackle first."

"Why don't you tell me about yourself, as much as you feel comfortable sharing."

With these words, Charlie set the stage for an hour of listening to the troublesome life experiences of Jim Allgood. He could have begun with a gospel question, but Charlie felt he had to know something about Jim before he could share his faith or offer specific direction.

Guidance as Person-Centered

In our contrast of styles we have demonstrated the two starting points. The confrontational model, such as Evangelism Explosion, begins with the gospel and communicates its truth to persons with an invitation to accept Christ and begin living for Christ. The relational approach begins with a person's narrative and seeks to discern the presence of God in it and to stimulate the person's imagination with a witness, either personal or scriptural.

Both approaches can be found in the biblical narratives. In the case of the leper, Jesus began with the leper's need. "If you will, you can make me clean," said the leper.

Jesus responded, "I will; be clean" (Mark 1:40–41).

In the case of the Samaritan woman, Jesus began in her context. The initial contact began with a request: "Give me a drink" (John 4:7). In making the request, Jesus entered into her world, gave her control of the relation, and through her service enhanced her self-esteem.

In another instance Philip engaged the Ethiopian eunuch in the eunuch's context. When Philip joined the eunuch, his first question was, "Do you understand what you are reading?" (Acts 8:30). The question provided the setting for the eunuch to request help. In response, Philip spoke to him of Christ.

Jesus' address to his disciples and the crowd illustrates the direct approach. The scripture states, "Then said Jesus to the crowds and to his disciples, 'The scribes and the Pharisees sit on Moses' seat; so practice and observe whatever they tell you, but not what they do; for they preach, but do not practice' " (Matt. 23:1–3).

Peter demonstrates a directness in his address to the multitude on the day of Pentecost. His sermon ended with the affirmation of the Lordship of Christ. When the people heard his message, they were convinced of the person of Jesus and asked, "What shall we do?"

Peter responded directly: "Repent, and be baptized every one of you in the name of Jesus Christ for the forgiveness of your sins; and you shall receive the gift of the Holy Spirit" (Acts 2:38).

Paul demonstrated the same directness with the Philippian jailer. The earthquake had shattered the security system; the jailer faced execution if one prisoner escaped. Fearing the worst, he was about to commit suicide. Paul cried out, "Do not harm yourself for we are all here!"

Immediately the jailer asked, "What must I do to be saved?"

Paul responded, "Believe in the Lord Jesus, and you will be saved; you and your household" (Acts 16:28, 30–31).

These references support the contention that spiritual guidance may begin either with the gospel or with the person. If both have scriptural legitimacy, why have we strongly emphasized the person-centered approach?

The person-centered approach shows a respect for the individual; to begin guidance with the person's experience and history communicates an interest in the whole person, not just the salvation of the soul. Beginning in this fashion also helps the guide to resist indoctrination as a means of evangelism.

This bias toward persons presupposes the prior activity of God in their life. In too many instances the direct approach ignores the history of God's work by treating the subject as an alien. This blindness leads to discounting the person's life before the moment of conversion; it provides no help in reevaluating the past and integrating it into the person's ongoing life.

When a guide intentionally listens, the guide expects to hear God in the person's life. Hearing the narrative not only points to the action of the Spirit, the narrative calls forth the appropriate gospel truth. Without this concentration on the subject, the guide administers the same prescription to everyone. This unimaginative strategy not only severely limits the spiritual guide, it violates the creative style of Christ, who seemed to have a fresh appeal for every individual.

The person-centered approach furthermore places confidence in the free, redemptive power of the Spirit. God has novel approaches to bring Christ to human consciousness. In some sense the Word of God has been planted unidentified in the memory of the subject through previous encounters. Recounting past experiences provides an opportunity for the spiritual guide to identify that presence with words. Making the identification of the Spirit in a person's narrative and speaking words is a witness with a powerful impact.

Suppose a person who has a vague awareness of God describes to the guide an experience of crisis. "When my mother was seriously ill, I recall a time when peace came to me; I felt a strength other than my own sustaining me."

In response the guide says, "I believe God gives us that kind of strength when we come to the edge of our own ability." The narrative of the witness contains a "word of God"; the witness identifies that "word" and speaks it back so that the person hears it from his or her own experience. In no sense does this make the biblical word irrelevant or unnecessary. The biblical message provides the norm by which the guide discerns and proclaims the word incarnate in the journeyer.

This person-centered approach does not depend on mental assent, as does the confrontational model, but trusts in the Spirit to create a new center of awareness and thus a new center of power. The Spirit enables the imagination to take the creative leap from a flat world of the senses into the dimension of the Spirit. The gospel informs this transformation with the life and teaching of Christ.

We believe this approach demonstrates a deeper faith in the Spirit to continue to work in an individual after the face-to-face encounter. If the good seeds of the gospel have been sown and cultivated, the Spirit will continue to nurture them; therefore, we do not feel forced to press for an immediate decision. This style does not lend itself to "scalp counting" because any encounter or conversation with another is but one event in their ongoing life journey. Every person's life has a "before" and an "after"; no single experience can mark the end of the faith journey.

Guidance as Process

A person's completed relationship with God does not occur in an instant, maybe not in a lifetime. Rather, the relation with God develops like a marriage—through courtship, ceremony, and a lifetime of learning to enjoy and appreciate each other. Dallas Willard suggests that salvation is not just forgiveness but a new order of life. To be saved surely means more than a mental transaction of "Yes, I believe in Jesus Christ as my personal savior." Willard says, "One specific errant concept has done inestimable harm to the church and God's purposes with us—and that is the concept that has restricted the Christian idea of salvation to *mere forgiveness of sins.*"[1]

In contrast, the life of a Christian consists of being conformed to the image of Christ. As in a marriage, the courtship provides the prelude in which the affections are awakened by the Spirit, the vows mark a transition from courtship to marriage, and the relationship matures after the ceremony.

Willard puts the issue succinctly: "The one lesson we learn from all available sources is that there is no 'quick fix' for the human condition. The approach to wholeness is for humankind a process of great length and difficulty and engages all our powers to their fullest extent over a long course of experience."[2]

Viewing evangelism as initial spiritual guidance has caused us to focus on the "mutual discovery and courtship" phase of the divine-human relationship. This prelude to significant commitment occurs over a period of time. The following interview indicates several stages in this process.

The minister, Warren Gray, met with a couple in his office for premarital counseling. Dan had been reared in the church but had drifted away from it. Helen, his high school sweetheart, had recently become a Christian and was enthusiastic about her faith. Dan's mother regularly attended church, but his father seldom came. Helen attended with her future mother-in-law.

The couple came to the office after work. Following a period of light conversation, Warren moved to discuss matters of faith and marriage.

(1) "Helen, when you joined the church you told me a bit about your background, but could you tell me a little more about your church involvement?"

"When I was little we went to church regularly, but when I was about eight years old, my parents stopped going to church. My mother's parents were both ministers in a rather strict denomination."

(2) "You think she might have been reacting to some early rearing?"

"Probably."

"Go on with your story."

"After my parents stopped going to church, I went occasionally when I felt like it or when my friends asked me to go. I went to a youth group at the New London church, but when I went to college, I found a church I really liked."

Sensing Dan's discomfort, Warren briefly changed the subject and asked about how the two had met. They had been high school sweethearts, and so had Warren and his wife. They chatted about this similarity for a few minutes.

(1) "Dan, I wonder about your feelings toward the church, since your attendance has been a little sparse recently"—said with a smile and a warm voice.

"Yeah, Christmas and Easter, that's about it."

"What does the church mean to you at this point, especially as you think about marriage? Is there a relation between church and the quality of a marriage?

Dan struggled for words. "How do I say it? Not really. I think often about God, and I have my way of praying. But I don't like to mix with people too much. The church is important to Helen and I'm proud of her for going, but I really don't feel the need to be here."

"I'm sort of worried about unequal yoking," Helen blurted out.

Puzzled, Dan asked, "What's that?"

Warren explained. "I think Helen is referring to Paul's warning about a believer being married to an unbeliever."

"I believe in God. I think a lot about God. I just have my own way of praying, that's all."

With good discernment Warren responded.

(2) "I get the feeling that you may have been forced to come to church as a young person, so that when you were able to, you said goodbye to the church."

Smiling, Dan looked at Warren and wondered how he knew. "Yes, that's it. When I got a job, I could say I didn't have time to go. When I got older, I decided I liked lying in bed on Sunday. So I just stopped coming."

(3) "I can relate to that. I hated church from a young age. Church bored me; I was uncomfortable there and I had to associate with kids I didn't like all that much. Probably makes you wonder how I became a minister."

Warren continued.

(4) "Dan, I've observed a number of families; I note how significant persons have a strong influence on our lives. You have two strong role models in your grandparents, persons of deep faith and strong loyalty to the church.

"But it's different with your folks. Your mother comes faithfully, but your dad comes less now than when I first came as the minister. Is that a fair assessment?"

"I'd say so. Dad was here every week when we were growing up, but he's not that regular anymore."

"Do you ever feel the conflict in these two role models working inside you?"

"Yes, I do. I feel a pull in two different directions."

(5) "Dan, I'd like to invite you as an adult man to think about your relation to God and the church. You're grown now; you can choose what is important for your life, and

I hope you will let this issue be in your mind as we think about your upcoming marriage. Is that fair enough?"

"Sure."

This brief interview illustrates five stages in the process of guiding someone to faith or to a consideration of faith: discovery, discernment, disclosure, direction, and discipleship.

Each stage is numbered in the text of the interview.

Discovery: The guide's effort to discover the narrative

(1) *"Helen, when you joined the church you told me a bit about your background, but could you tell me a little more about your church involvement?"*

"Dan, I wonder about your feelings toward the church, since your attendance has been a little sparse recently."

In both inquiries Warren invited Helen and Dan to discover something about their relationship to the church. To use the church as a starting point posed less of a threat than asking about their relationship with God. Both of them could and did relate accurately their feelings about the church. Though Warren may have this information in his mind already, it strengthens the conversation for the couple to acknowledge it aloud.

Warren recognized the possible influence of Helen's and Dan's parents.

Discernment: The guide's discernment of the situation

(2) *"You think she might have been reacting to some early rearing?"*

"I get the feeling that you may have been forced to come to church as a young person, so that when you were able to, you said goodbye to the church."

In both these encounters, first with Helen and then with Dan, Warren demonstrated sensitive discernment. He imagined that Helen's mother stopped attending church because she felt oppression from the church of her childhood. He properly discerned that Dan's disinterest in the church stemmed from pressure on him as a child. Though it is never said, Dan and Helen's mother suffered from a similar problem—being forced to attend church.

Disclosure: The guide's disclosure to the subject

(3) *"I can relate to that. I hated church from a young age. Church bored me; I was uncomfortable there and I had to associate with kids I didn't like all that much. Probably makes you wonder how I became a minister."*

With this response Warren made an effort to identify with Dan. He shared part of himself with him. The disclosure could have been a passage of scripture instead of this witness from his own life.

Direction: The guide's direction of the subject

(4) *"Dan, I've observed a number of families; I note how significant persons have a strong influence on our lives. You have two strong role models in your grandparents, persons of deep faith and strong loyalty to the church."*

With this statement Warren subtly held up images of Christian faith and dedication. In this act he invited Dan to consider the role model of his grandparents as one appropriate for himself.

Discipleship: The guide's invitation to change

(5) *"Dan, I'd like to invite you as an adult man to think about your relation to God and the church. You're grown now; you can choose what is important for your life, and I hope you will let this issue be in your mind as we think about your upcoming marriage. Is that fair enough?"*

This was a simple, clear invitation appropriate to Dan's situation. True, a more direct confrontation could have occurred, but this was the first counseling session and Warren knew that Dan would be around after the wedding. No need to create a barrier by pressing too hard in the first meeting.

This basic five-part process defines the necessary movements or stages in a conversation with a person about faith. The content of the question and the response will vary with each individual, but most conversations will include most if not all of these elements.

Pitfalls

Having looked at some of the inadequacies of other approaches in guiding persons in the first steps of faith, it is appropriate now to identify the pitfalls that this approach may have. Perhaps a case could be made for leaving out this list of warnings. In an hour when the church desperately needs courage to "speak the faith" to persons and has demonstrated its reluctance to engage persons in significant conversations in which faith is born, does not a list of problems weaken the advocacy? Perhaps. But to ignore these problems would be both dishonest and unfaithful.

Those committed to this basic task of ministry must know the traps awaiting the faithful guide. The knowledge of obstacles should make the guide alert and wise. Wisdom and a degree of maturity will save us from the abuses of such an important ministry.

But how does a person beginning this ministry get wisdom, sensitivity, and maturity? Is it not by actually guiding persons into a faith relationship with Christ? It seems to be a "Catch-22" situation. Spiritual guidance can best be done by experienced persons, but how do we get experience except by guiding others into the faith?

Perhaps parenting provides an analogy to the ministry of guidance. With the first child, parents have no experience in child rearing. They gain experience by having children and bringing them up. Becoming a spiritual guide creates risks like those involved in daring to have children. Here are some pitfalls that spiritual guides, as parents in the faith, must guard against.

Discouragement

One of the first and most persistent temptations to attack the guide is discouragement. Consider a woman who feels called to this ministry. She prepares herself through study and prayer. One day in conversation with a fellow worker, the friend says, "My life hasn't been going the way I had hoped."

The guide picks up on the clue and asks, "How do you mean?" Her interest leads to a long conversation. But when the guide asks about her faith, the troubled person changes the subject and quickly suggests they had better get back to work.

The guide wonders what she did wrong, how she failed, and what different tack to take next time. This early turn-off may confirm her worst fear—rejection. Her response to this encounter could have taken a dozen forms, but given her personality and her experience, she falls into discouragement.

Stories of discouragement have a thousand characters: persons who come very near a commitment to Christ; persons who resist making a choice; those who begin and turn back to old ways; those in whom hours have been invested to no avail. Some never show any signs of appreciation, and some even discount the faith of the witness.

Is this not the way of parenthood? Children rarely take the exact course their parents have dreamed of. Can any parent claim to have reared children without becoming discouraged at some point?

We must remember that birthing new life is God's business, not ours. Jesus' description of the soils indicates that the receptivity of the person also provides an important ingredient. I wonder how Jesus felt about his whole life's work on the morning after the resurrection. Not a single disciple had remained faithful. Can we rightfully expect our ministry of love to be free of discouragement?

Feelings of Inadequacy

Has any person ever engaged in this task without serious feelings of inadequacy? Whenever the person with even modest self-doubt pauses to consider the task in which he or she engages, surely the enormity of it must seem staggering. How can one mortal help another become connected to God?

Imagine it! A human being offering mind, body, history, and experience to conduct the Spirit of God. In the conversation, in the relationship, in the feelings of love and concern, in the biblical narrative we tell, we are hoping that the living God will transmit that saving presence to another person through us. "Through us!" That is the basis of the inadequacy; can our life become a conductor of the divine presence?

But do not all who give birth feel this? Do parents ever feel adequate for the task?

What must have been going through the soul of Paul when he cried out, "Who is sufficient for these things?" In his letter to the Corinthians, Paul acknowledged the difficulty of being an apostle and bearing witness for Christ. Yet in the midst of his struggles, he felt gratitude to God who, in Christ, always led him triumphantly. Contemplating this very issue, he said, "We are the aroma of Christ to God among those who are being saved and among those who are perishing, to one a fragrance from death to death, to the other a fragrance from life to life." And then he staggers us with this question: "Who is sufficient for these things?" (2 Cor. 2:15–16). In that moment Paul expresses the inadequacy that every faithful follower of Christ must feel when seeking to touch the life of another.

A False Sense of Self

Call it pride if you wish! A guide's lack of personal or spiritual maturity creates fertile soil in which vanity takes root and grows. Without a thorough knowledge of oneself, the gratitude and praise of a newly awakened person gets the guide out of focus. She or he begins to believe the affirmations of greatness made by the excited new Christian. The adulation of a person who has been greatly helped seems to be spontaneous and universal, like the love of a child for its mother.

As guides, we often do not need the praise of another to

stimulate our pride. We can generate it ourselves. Some deficiency, some quirk in our nature or hunger for recognition, causes us to think that our efforts have made possible the transformation of another. Whether caused by ourself or another, the loss of focus on Christ leads to unwarranted pride. In the grip of pride, we lose perspective and engage in a good task for the wrong reasons.

Ignatius had a terrifying image for the guide who falls into pride. He said, "They are like hunting dogs who eat the hare, rather than bringing it to the master."

The mission group of the seventy faced the same temptation. They returned from their first preaching journey saying that "even the demons are subject to us." Quickly Jesus corrected them. "Do not rejoice in this, that the spirits are subject to you; but rejoice that your names are written in heaven" (Luke 10:17, 20).

Parents sometimes seek their own identity and feelings of worth in their children's performance. If the children succeed, they feel good about themselves. If they fail, the parents feel wiped out. The spiritual guide must seek to avoid this pitfall.

Surely the guide must keep a sense of perspective on this ministry. A clear perspective requires vigilance in resisting pride.

Spiritualism

The role of a "connector" is supercharged. How could a person be standing beside another who has recently been infused with the Spirit of Christ and not feel the afterglow! Encounters with the Spirit have a certain lure. The ecstasy, the joyous delight in God, often turns persons from the basic task of witness and guidance to a lust for spiritual experience.

The spiritual guide who becomes enticed by the effects of the Spirit places his or her attention at the wrong point. This focus leads directly to Gnosticism, an ancient perversion of the gospel that used secret knowledge, rituals, and spiritual techniques to produce spiritual experience.

Lured by that heresy, the spiritual guide pretends a special knowledge of the Spirit's work and leads persons into experiences of his or her own making.

The faithful guide clearly issues the call of Christ and invites persons to respond; he or she does not produce spiritual experiences. Jesus Christ alone takes charge of the divine-human meeting.

In the family, parents give birth to children, not primarily for their own pleasure but to share life with them. When parents place their own delight above the fulfillment of the children, the children always suffer. So it is with the spiritual guide and the children of faith.

Professionalism

Perhaps the worst thing that can happen to a spiritual guide is to become a professional; it erases dependence on God. The guide's strategy, the plan of salvation, or the special technique usurps the place of the living presence of Christ in the professional. Plans and strategies are not excluded, but they must not be divorced from a deep sensitivity to the divine Presence; they make poor substitutes for the Presence.

The telltale symptoms of professionalism appear when guides depend on their technique to introduce persons to faith, when they treat persons like objects and manipulate them toward their own ends, when they lose touch with their own souls and forget why they got involved in this ministry. These symptoms begin to appear when the guides think they "know how" to guide persons to faith.

Guides who "know how" no longer expect the unexpected. No surprises can break in upon them because they have taken control of the relation and have left no room for the Spirit of Christ.

Look at the ministry of Jesus, for example. He encounters every person differently: his approach is ever new, his metaphors are fresh, his style is adapted to the occasion. In the Gospel of Mark, to cite just one source, Jesus uses thirty-nine different ways to communicate the love of God to persons—novel, unique, open to the moment.

Three directions are in order. Remember that every person will bring a new challenge, steadily resist the illusion that you "know how" to do this ministry, and keep an openness to the Spirit's work in your own life.

Limited Vision

Initial spiritual guidance marks the beginning of a person's journey. The guide serves as a midwife. The delivery of a baby marks a new beginning of parenthood, not the end.

Like a faithful parent, the spiritual guide must provide nurture and care for the newly awakened person. The greatest gift may be availability. The newly born need to know that someone is there, available for them, both for their questions and their failures.

New believers must learn about the faith and begin developing the disciplines of worship, prayer, and Bible study—disciplines that will sustain them in times of testing and deepen their faith for effective ministry.

All the newly born need nourishment and care.

Sources of Help

Where can the guide find help? Each spiritual guide needs a peer group of guides with whom to share experiences. This group provides both support and valuable correction.

A spiritual guide needs guidance. Perhaps a spiritual director for each guide would be advisable. This director would make guides accountable.

The spiritual guide requires continuous training to deepen understanding, refine discernment, and sharpen skills. These special training events provide new insights into the gospel, other persons, and the nature of the task.

Parents read books on how to raise children, they bring wisdom from their own experience, but they often fail. When they fail, they do not cease to be parents. They must, no matter how hard, begin the task again. No limit has been set on the number of times parents can begin again.

Is not the same true for the spiritual guide?

10

Toward A Reformed Church

Our efforts to this point have been directed toward a single problem: How can we find courage, conviction, and a course of action that will enable us to speak directly to persons about God? The focus has been on one individual helping another. Now this most basic unit of ministry must be set in the context of the church. What does this form of ministry mean for the congregation? How can a concerned minister make the congregation a community of spiritual guides?

I seek to address the leadership of America's mainline churches. My deepest hope is to spell out a vision that will fire the pastor's imagination with new possibilities for ministry. If a few persons have a renewal of faith, that energy has the potential to impact the congregation and, through the congregation, the denomination. Like many pastors I dream of my denomination becoming vital and alive through the Spirit, being truly open to all, inclusive of theological, economic, and social diversity, and giving as much attention to conversion and commitment as it does to compassion and justice.

To make such a vision a reality, we must begin where we are, with the membership now in our churches. None would question that our churches have countless numbers of devout and faithful souls. Most of them have reached the sixth decade of life. Soon they will become less active and more limited in their giving and in their ministry.

In addition to this large group of faithful members, our church has a small percentage of persons who make no claim to a personal relationship to Jesus Christ. They, of course, believe in God and the church, but they do not speak personally of Christ, nor are they seriously engaged in mission. Too often their faith has been shaped by a culture that values health, wealth, and success.

In our churches, too many pastors have a built-in resistance to speaking one-to-one about personal faith, either theirs or others'. Lay men and women sense this lack but often do not know how to put their perception into words. Pastors themselves feel an emptiness and a lack of focus, making them cherish all the more the memory of those noble dreams when they first decided for the ministry.

I do not intend to indict the clergy and convict us without a trial. Not every clergy member feels this reluctance or struggles with this handicap, but far too many of us do experience the paradox of being spokespersons for God and yet uncertain of what to say. In some creative fashion we must address this situation of nominal laity and speechless clergy if the church is to be revitalized.

One of the issues that must be directly addressed is the church's agenda. For the past two and a half decades, social and political issues have headed the priority lists of the major denominations. The emphasis, according to the year, has shifted from poverty to unemployment, to abortion, to gay rights, to the sanctuary movement, to liberation in the Third World, to disarmament. Without question these issues must be addressed by the Christian community, but not to the exclusion of introducing persons to faith in Christ.

While engaged in these issues of a social and corporate nature, words like "personal," "spiritual," and "conversion" have been little used in the denominational vocabulary. In an effort to be universally relevant, we have often forgotten about individuals both inside and outside the church who need to be introduced to a personal faith. The analysis of American culture as individualistic has served to make intellectuals even more uninterested in personal conversion.

From many quarters, the only word to draw more fire than "personal" is the word "spiritual." This term often smacks of an inward-looking religion, a retreat from the world, perhaps a focus on self-realization. When will we learn that "spiritual" has to do with the consciousness of God—God's call and our response to it? I sometimes fear that the church has overreacted to the "spirituality of the church" heresy, which limits the church's voice to matters of the soul and thereby excludes economics and politics. The church rightly rejected this bifurcation of the gospel into spiritual and material, sacred and secular. But in rejecting the spirituality of the church, it seems to have eliminated all interest in spirituality.

The hour has come to birth an inclusive spirituality that gives proper grounding both to our evangelistic witness and our concern for justice. Unless both these facets of mission are grounded in the consciousness of God's call, one degenerates into church growth without life and the other into political lobbying without Christian substance. Our churches must come anew to an awareness of the "God who is," who comes to us and calls us into the mission of the kingdom.

"Conversion," it often seems, has also been written in the life of the church with disappearing ink. Without personal conversion, either of the nurtured or the dramatic type, the church lacks the energy to fulfill its mission. Nothing takes the place of conversion—neither training, nor service, nor membership. Personal conversion to the Lordship of Jesus Christ, which issues in a holistic spirituality, is required if the church is to have the power and stamina to fulfill its world-changing mission.

Westerhoff makes a telling point. "We can nurture persons into institutional religion, but not into mature Christian faith. The Christian faith by its very nature demands conversion."[1] The urgent need throughout the mainline churches seems to me to be personal conversion to Jesus Christ.

Do we not sense the crisis in the contemporary church? We have an adult membership that needs personal conversion and a clergy embarrassed, anxious, or for some reason inept at speaking personally about God. Where does this dilemma place the church?

Must there not be an awakening or a conversion of the church, both clergy and laity? I use the word "conversion" in its generic sense—turning toward God, letting ourselves be turned in repentance by God's call. In every corner of the church a few persons witness to a movement of God in their lives. Clergy, too! Not long ago, a minister who graduated from an eastern school, a man deeply concerned for peace and justice in the world, said, "I can say this to you and you will understand. For the first time in my ministry I have a personal relationship with Jesus Christ." Personal awakenings like this must combine to form small rivulets, which unite to form a torrent of renewal that refreshes the whole church.

Can It Be?

I spoke with a longtime friend of mine about the state of the church.

"Do you think we will be able to turn the church around?" I asked.

"No. The statistics don't seem to indicate it. The only hope we have is a miracle from God." He spoke with a note of optimism, as though he believed it might happen.

What shape would a miracle of God take that combined spiritual guidance with the task of evangelism? If we should experience the miracle of a divine visitation, it might result in a new understanding of ministry. Perhaps we would be grasped by God deeply enough to realize that the call of God constitutes the foundation of ministry—called by God to believe in and to re-present Christ. This dynamic tension between God's call and our response would issue in a lifestyle of obedience. This personal encounter with God would result in a balanced agenda for our churches.

With new vision, the minister would see the laity not as a threat but as fellow members in the body of Christ, coworkers in the kingdom of God. The minister might begin listening to those persons who are seeking spiritual nurture and encouragement. If the minister felt unprepared, he or she might begin a personal search.

But How?

The recognition of need, often coupled with feelings of desperation, has spread widely across the church. Many are willing to try a different approach, but what approach will it be? Numerous strategies offer to help us to "begin at the beginning." Which one shall we take?

Some months ago I was invited to conduct a workshop in the Pittsburgh Presbytery of the Presbyterian Church (U.S.A.). One of the members of the host committee invited me to speak at his church, the Pleasant Hills Community Church. "My pastor will appreciate your words," he said. Little did I realize that just the reverse would be the case—I would appreciate the pastor's words.

My host invited the ministerial staff, a few friends, and me for an early dinner before I spoke to a gathering of the church. Before the meal I began an acquaintance with E. Stanley Ott, the senior minister. I could tell from his response to my questions, his nods of agreement when I spoke, and an occasional smile that we had a great deal in common.

When the dinner ended, we made our way to the church. That evening as I spoke, the expression on Stan's face told me that he and I were in sync. After the people had spoken graciously to me, and he and I were in his office, he reached up to a shelf, pulled out a book, and handed it to me. The book was entitled *The Vital Church,* and on the spine was the author's name, E. Stanley Ott.

On my trip home the next day I reached into my briefcase, pulled out the book, and began reading. It read like a Robert Ludlum novel—clear, concise, fast-paced, intriguing, revealing. After reading the first ten pages I knew why Stan's face had lit up during my talk; he had already spelled out in this book the kind of dream for the church that I was describing to his people.

I do not think he has all the answers to our dilemma. His book certainly does not hold the only answer, but it does describe a clear vision of the vibrant church, and it gives specific strategies which, through the grace of God, can help make it happen.

A Vibrant Church

"Every church can be a vibrant church!" So says Stan Ott. He sees two ways to revitalize the church—through the renewal of individuals and the renewal of the church's vision and structure—and both are important for a vital congregation.

In most instances it is necessary to begin the renewal process with individuals in their personal faith and discipleship. Renewed individuals without a renewed structure face discouragement, and the situation also frustrates the pastoral leader. But to try to renew the organization without the renewed faith of individuals results in death. Whether or not you change the positions of the bodily parts of a corpse, it is still a corpse.[2]

What makes a vibrant congregation? Vibrant persons do, persons whose lives have been touched by the Spirit of Christ; persons who find nurture in worship, prayer, and the study of God's word; persons who have established a base of fellowship and support; persons who engage in witness and ministries of justice. To presume to have a vital congregation that does not have members with spiritual sensitivity and a depth of commitment to Christ is to live with an illusion.

To develop persons with these characteristics requires intentional pastoral leadership. The pastoral role is more than the ministry of Word and Sacrament, more than pastoral care, more than trying to do all the ministry. Effective pastoral leaders have a purpose—such as the congregation being vibrant with the life of Christ, reproducing that life, and expressing it in the church's particular context. Effective leaders have a plan—a strategy for helping the church become a vibrant body of Christ. But to be effective, leaders must have followers, persons who share the vision and participate in the mission. Ministers must always have a double focus: the individual and the community of faith. While ministers respond to individual persons, they also keep as a priority the spirit of love in the church and a clear focus of the corporate witness of the church.

In order to have mature individuals and an effective congregational ministry, we must focus on the person and the community. The twin focus of reaching individuals and renewing the congregation provides an appropriate setting for initial spiritual guidance.

Toward a Mature Christian

At the personal level the church aims to produce mature Christian men and women who share significantly in the ministry of Jesus Christ. Mature Christians have a "new self," a self characterized by a new spirit from Christ, a new mind, and a new lifestyle. To become a Christian means to receive from God the renewing grace of Christ, a grace that creates a new center of consciousness out of which life is lived. This new center in our lives develops as we grow in love for God and love for our neighbor and share in the ministry of witness to the world.

Since Christians do not mature overnight, it is essential to have a vision both of the goal and of the principles needed to guide our ministry in developing persons. Ott identifies five "people-building principles" to guide our work with those persons who have been awakened to new life in Christ. These five principles are prayer, care, "with me," the word, and "send them."

Christians cannot mature without prayer, a regular disciplined time of daily communion with God. Persons in the fellowship of Christ need both to give and receive care; care speaks of encouragement, support, fellowship. The "with me" principle has roots in Jesus' method of training by association. Jesus "appointed twelve, to be with him" (Mark 3:14). This "with me" principle finds practical expression in "Come, go to church with me"; "Join with me in a prayer group"; "Go with me to build the house for Habitat for Humanity." If persons are to catch the faith, they must be "with" persons who have the faith. The word of scripture provides the guidance and inspiration necessary for the Christian. "Let the word of Christ dwell in you richly, as you teach and admonish one another in all wisdom, and as you sing psalms and hymns and spiritual songs with thankfulness in your hearts to God" (Col. 3:16). The "send them" principle has its grounding in Jesus' appointing of the twelve "to be sent out to preach" (Mark 3:14).

These principles guide the minister in building a cadre of persons to share in the ministry of Christ; they also guide the individual in his or her ministry to other persons. Each of these principles offers a way for effective ministry. Perhaps the best setting to utilize these principles is in a small group.

Toward a Vibrant Congregation

A vibrant congregation consists of vital Christians who live the new life in Christ, but the renewal of a congregation requires more than individual renewal. I very much like the analogy Ott draws of the congregation and an orchestra; it must have individuals (like the musicians), but it also requires **leadership** (like the conductor), **bonding** factors (every musician committed to the orchestra), **nesting** structures that perform different ministries (strings, woodwinds, percussion, brass), and **knowledge and style** (conductor and musicians share a common knowledge of music and work together to produce a symphony). These four factors—leadership, bonding, nesting, and informed lifestyle—constitute the essentials for building vibrant congregational life.[3]

Leadership is essential. Just as an orchestra would be in disarray without a conductor, a church cannot function well without a leader. The congregation must be bonded together; unity grows as members deepen their relation to Christ, to each other, and to the shared vision of mission. Nesting refers to units required in revitalizing a congregation—the individual, the small group, the community of committed disciples, and the whole church. The ultimate goal is to make the whole congregation a vital community. In congregations like the Church of the Saviour in Washington, D.C., a high level of commitment, plus informed discipleship, have made the renewal groups synonymous with the membership of the church.

Stan Ott offers sage advice for anyone who wishes to begin the work of renewal in a congregation: "Find your few."[4] Begin with those persons who are willing to venture into growth. No matter how large the congregation, it is necessary for the pastor to focus on a few persons, to disciple them as a nucleus for ministry. But while focusing on the few, the minister sustains the ministry to the many through public worship, teaching, phone calls, and counseling. And as the few disciples mature, they begin to participate in the work, relieving the minister's load.

Congregation revitalization demands a plan. When we evaluate the worship, instruction, fellowship, and expression (mission) of the congregation, we can spot those areas in which need exists. From this need awareness, the committees of the church develop strategies and implement them in ways that begin to transform the church into a vibrant body of Christ.

For those of us who have struggled with old, staid, rigid congregations, there is hope. God does not will the church to sink into oblivion but to be revitalized by the Spirit. A committed ministry with the will to work, pray, and trust God can lead the congregation into a new vision for life. None of us can afford to sink into despair and settle for the status quo.

The Spiritual Guide

The vision for ministry we have described addresses the minister who wishes to give priority to the basic task of ministry—helping a person come to personal faith in Jesus Christ. Whether the minister's deficiency in performing this task has come about through a negative reaction to stereotypes of evangelism, a lack of spiritual formation, a theological framework suspect of religious experience, or the seduction of the therapeutic, many of us mainline ministers need help in guiding persons to faith in Christ.

Each of us must begin this retooling by exploring our

own faith experience, claiming the validity of our particular pathway to personal faith, and discovering our unique style of communicating faith to others. This personal exploration by the minister must precede giving vital leadership in creating the "vibrant church."

All that we have written about the theological perspective, the style, the search for meaning, stages of consciousness, discernment, and making the connection offers insight into how the minister begins to work with "the few" who will share the ministry. These same principles and strategies apply to the lay persons who guide others into faith and assist them in their commitment.

The Final Challenge

There is a correspondence between the missionary work on a foreign field and the work done in the churches of the Western world. Lesslie Newbigin suggests that the task in the West may be even more difficult than mission in a foreign culture. Of our culture, he says, "It is a pagan society, and its paganism, having been born out of the rejection of Christianity, is far more resistant to the gospel than the pre-Christian paganism with which cross-cultural missions have been familiar. Here, surely, is the most challenging missionary frontier of our time."[5]

To mount this Christian offensive in our postmodern culture, which has the character of cross-cultural missions, I would like to see the mainline churches respond to the challenge put forth by Vincent J. Donovan, a Roman Catholic missionary to Africa. About twenty-five years ago he went to the Loliondo Mission in East Africa to work among the Masai. After about a year he assessed the situation as desperate. He reviewed the history of the mission, which had begun over a hundred years ago. To get the work started, the missionaries had bought slaves from the slave dealers. They envisioned teaching them in their school, helping them develop skills, and getting them jobs. They hoped to arrange marriages, baptize their children, and gradually build an enormous body of believers. The actual number of converts after one hundred years was negligible.

From the beginning their method had questionable motives; it required subservience and dependence on the mission; the mission itself often looked with condescension upon the people; and, as a whole, the missionary work was distorted. Over the years the mission developed a number of schools, which taught the faith but used secular teachers as catechists. At one point teachers were told to build up the schools, if a conflict existed between the schools and religion. The central question "What is the purpose of missionary work?" never seemed to be addressed.

Following the Second World War the African leadership called on the mission for help. A new type of missionary developed, walking behind the plow, laying pipe, importing miracle grain, digging wells—an ecclesiastical Peace Corps. The mission work, which was born in slavery and later disoriented by the school system, had now been startled by independence and smothered by nation-building.

Finding this situation in 1966 Donovan said, "To make any sense out of mission . . . one has to start all over again—at the beginning." With that decision he wrote to the bishop and summarized his findings. There were four schools, a chapel, and a hospital, all of which took enormous time and energy. The Masai people had been helped materially by the mission, but when priests visited the villages, religion was hardly ever mentioned. The best description of the effect of the mission was the number zero—no adult practicing Christians, no children remaining in the faith after school days—and the religious life of the Masai was dismal.

In light of this painful assessment of the mission, Donovan wrote to the bishop, "I am weary of all the discussion about strategy. . . . I suddenly feel the urgent need

. . . to go to these people and do the work among them for which I came to Africa. I propose to go . . . and talk to them about God and the Christian message. . . . I want to go to the Masai in daily safaris unencumbered with the burden of selling them on our school system or begging them for their children for our schools or carrying their sick or giving them medicine. . . . Outside of this I have no theory, no plan, no strategy, no gimmicks—no idea of what will come. I feel rather naked. I will begin as soon as possible."[6]

Donovan's strategy was simple. He proposed to go directly to the people with the story of Christ. On his first visit to one of the tribes, he explained that he wanted to talk about God in the life of the Masai. He said that "it was for this very work of explaining the message of Christianity to the different people of Africa that I came here from far away."

The old chief looked at him for a long time and innocently asked, "If that is why you came here, why did you wait so long to tell us about this?"

After struggling for an answer, Donovan satisfied the old chief and gained permission to talk with the people. He found himself standing before them with nothing but the gospel of Christ—no medicine, no books, no bribes of any sort, just the naked gospel.

He said, "If I fail here I might as well go home."[7]

He resolved that he had nothing to give but Christ. With this decision he began going to each tribe, presenting the gospel, and leaving them for a period to decide on their response. When the response was positive, he baptized the people, appointed leaders, and went on. His efforts were part of a great spiritual awakening in East Africa.

After reflecting on his experience, Vincent Donovan wrote, "I wonder if you ever reach that point in your life or in your work where you are certain that you will never have to start all over again."[8]

Does it ever seem to you that we have forgotten what the church is for? Have we become enamored with education, good works of compassion, equality of persons, and justice for all to the point that we have lost sight of that most basic unit of Christianity—one person speaking to another of Christ? This challenge falls heavily upon American mainline churches in particular. Like the African example, nothing we are doing can be called "bad," but we seem not to address the deepest ache in the heart of the church or of the world. As a consequence the young have lost interest in our churches, and many who worship each week leave with unfulfilled lives.

I often feel in my own soul the kind of ache that Donovan described as he looked at the work of his church in East Africa. My church has done so many things well—buildings, budgets, education, ministries of compassion, a concern for justice—but as I look at the life of particular congregations, they often lack vitality. When I talk with lay persons and clergy, both groups confirm their hunger for God and their confusion as to what to do.

Many of us feel the challenge to "begin again at the beginning." What would happen if we went to people with nothing but the gospel, nothing but Jesus Christ? What if we met with our people and inquired of their relation to Christ, much as Richard Baxter did several centuries ago? Would this not shock most of our congregations? Yet the need cries out, and the possible rewards are worth the risks.

I wonder what would happen in our churches if for one year we canceled all committee meetings and the minister visited personally with each officer and asked two questions: "Tell me, if you will, what does Jesus Christ mean in your life?" And, "As the body of Christ, what do you think we should do together?"

After listening to their responses, what if the minister engaged the officers in interviewing each member of the congregation with the same two questions?

I have a notion these conversations would release more energy than the congregation could absorb and create visions that would transform our tired churches into a resurrected body of Christ!

Notes

Full publishing information not presented here appears in the Bibliography.

1: God-Speech: A Crisis in Evangelism

1. For a comprehensive discussion of this transition see E. Brooks Holifield, *A History of Pastoral Care in America.*
2. From a response to my analysis of our situation made by John Patton, Professor of Pastoral Care, Columbia Theological Seminary.
3. See a discussion on this issue in Wade C. Roof and William McKinney, *American Mainline Religion,* pp. 72–105.
4. A point made expressly by Robert Bellah et al. in *Habits of the Heart,* pp. 142–163.
5. Kenneth Leech, *Soul Friend,* p. iv.
6. William A. Barry and William J. Connolly, *The Practice of Spiritual Direction,* p. 8.
7. Morton T. Kelsey, *Companions on the Inner Way,* p. 7.
8. Leech, p. 37.

2: The Spiritual Guide Through the Ages

1. Richard Wilbur, "For Dudley," *Walking to Sleep* (New York: Harcourt Brace Jovanovich, 1971), p. 25.
2. Adapted from Urban Holmes, *The Priest in Community,* pp. 20–21.
3. Holmes, p. 13.
4. Holmes, p. 67.
5. Holmes, pp. 35–67.
6. Don S. Browning, *The Moral Context of Pastoral Care,* p. 45.
7. Browning, p. 47.

8. Cited in Michael Green, *Evangelism in the Early Church,* p. 172.
9. Cited in M. Green, p. 203.
10. Henri Nouwen, *The Way of the Heart,* pp. 14–15.
11. Richard Baxter, *The Reformed Pastor* (London: Epworth Press, 1939), p. 21.
12. E. Brooks Holifield, *A History of Pastoral Care in America,* p. 12.
13. Among these are Morton Kelsey, Kenneth Leech, Tilden Edwards, William Barry, William Connolly, and Gerald May.
14. For example, John Patton, Charles Gerkin, and Don Browning are making an effort to reclaim pastoral care for the church.
15. Tilden Edwards, *Spiritual Friend.*
16. Frances de Sales, *Introduction to the Devout Life* (Garden City, N.Y.: Doubleday & Co., Image Books), pp. 46–47.
17. Morton Kelsey, *Companions on the Inner Way.*

3: The Theological Structure of Spiritual Guidance

1. Reuben Job and Norman Shawchuck, *Prayers for Ministers and Other Servants,* p. 102.
2. For further amplification of personal narrative, see pp. 20–47 in Ben Campbell Johnson, *To Will God's Will.*
3. See the discussion in Ben Campbell Johnson, *Rethinking Evangelism,* pp. 32–34.
4. Ana-Maria Rizzuto, *Birth of the Living God* (Chicago: University of Chicago Press, 1979).

4: The Style of the Spiritual Guide

1. D. James Kennedy, *Evangelism Explosion,* p. 8.
2. Kennedy, p. 21.
3. William Barry and William J. Connolly, *The Practice of Spiritual Direction,* p. 46.
4. Ibid.

5: A Closer Look at the Person

1. J. Russell Hale, *Who Are the Unchurched?,* pp. 38–44.
2. Hale, p. 90.

3. Hale, p. 92.
4. Ibid.
5. Hale, p. 94.
6. Gerald G. May, *Addiction and Grace,* p. 1.
7. Charles V. Gerkin, *The Living Human Document,* chapters 6–8.
8. I have discussed this in *Rethinking Evangelism,* pp. 66–68.

6: A Faith-Awareness Spectrum

1. C. G. Jung, *Analytical Psychology: Its Theory and Practice;* note especially chapter 1.

7: The Role of Discernment

1. John H. Westerhoff III, *Will Our Children Have Faith?,* pp. 38–39.
2. Thomas Green, *Weeds Among the Wheat,* pp. 58–60.

8: Making the Connection

1. Garrett Green, *Imagining God,* pp. 41–80.
2. Thomas Kuhn, *The Structure of Scientific Revolutions* (Chicago: University of Chicago Press, 1978).
3. Cited in G. Green, p. 46.
4. Ibid., p. 77.
5. Ibid., p. 46.
6. Ibid., p. 19.
7. Kuhn, p. 158.
8. G. Green, p. 50.
9. Ibid., p. 54.
10. Ibid., p. 62.
11. Ibid., p. 69.
12. Ibid., p. 73.

9: Person, Process, and Pitfalls

1. Dallas Willard, *The Spirit of the Disciplines,* p. 33.
2. Willard, p. 70.

10: Toward a Reformed Church

1. John H. Westerhoff III, *Will Our Children Have Faith?,* p. 38.

2. E. Stanley Ott, *The Vibrant Church,* pp. 15, 16.
3. Ott, pp. 89–106.
4. Ott, p. 109.
5. Lesslie Newbigen, *Foolishness to the Greeks,* p. 20.
6. Vincent J. Donovan, *Christianity Rediscovered,* pp. 14–16.
7. Donovan, pp. 22, 23.
8. Donovan, p. 26.

Bibliography

Barry, William A., and William J. Connolly. *The Practice of Spiritual Direction*. New York: Seabury Press, 1982.

Bellah, Robert N., et al. *Habits of the Heart*. Berkeley, Calif.: University of California Press, 1985.

Browning, Don S. *The Moral Context of Pastoral Care*. Philadelphia: Westminster Press, 1976.

Donovan, Vincent J. *Christianity Rediscovered*. Maryknoll, N.Y.: Orbis Books, 1978.

Edwards, Tilden. *Spiritual Friend*. New York: Paulist Press, 1980.

Gerkin, Charles V. *The Living Human Document*. Nashville: Abingdon Press, 1984.

Green, Garrett. *Imagining God*. San Francisco: Harper & Row, 1989.

Green, Michael. *Evangelism in the Early Church*. Grand Rapids: Wm. B. Eerdmans Publishing Co., 1970.

Green, Thomas H., S.J. *Weeds Among the Wheat*. Notre Dame, Ind.: Ave Maria Press, 1984.

Hale, J. Russell. *Who Are the Unchurched?* Washington, D.C.: Glenmary Research Center, 1977.

Holifield, E. Brooks. *A History of Pastoral Care in America*. Nashville: Abingdon Press, 1983.

Holmes, Urban T., III. *The Priest in Community*. New York: Seabury Press, 1978.

Job, Reuben P., and Norman Shawchuck. *A Guide to Prayer*. Nashville: Upper Room, 1983.

Johnson, Ben Campbell. *Pastoral Spirituality.* Philadelphia: Westminster Press, 1988.

———. *Rethinking Evangelism.* Philadelphia: Westminster Press, 1983.

———. *To Pray God's Will.* Philadelphia: Westminster Press, 1987.

———. *To Will God's Will.* Philadelphia: Westminster Press, 1987.

Jung, C. G. *Analytical Psychology: Its Theory and Practice.* New York: Vintage Books, 1968.

Kelsey, Morton T. *Companions on the Inner Way.* New York: Crossroad Publishing Co., 1986.

Kennedy, D. James. *Evangelism Explosion.* Wheaton, Ill.: Tyndale House, 1970.

Leech, Kenneth. *Soul Friend.* San Francisco: Harper & Row, 1980.

May, Gerald G. *Addiction and Grace.* San Francisco: Harper & Row, 1988.

Nouwen, Henri J. M. *The Way of the Heart.* New York: Seabury Press, 1981.

Newbigen, Lesslie. *Foolishness to the Greeks.* Grand Rapids: Wm. B. Eerdmans Publishing Co., 1986.

Ott, E. Stanley. *The Vibrant Church.* Ventura, Calif.: Regal Books, 1989.

Robinson, Edward. *The Language of Mystery.* Philadelphia: Trinity Press International, 1987.

Roof, Wade Clark, and McKinney, William. *American Mainline Religion.* New Brunswick, N.J.: Rutgers University Press, 1987.

Westerhoff, John H., III. *Will Our Children Have Faith?* Minneapolis: Winston Press, 1976.

Willard, Dallas. *The Spirit of the Disciplines.* San Francisco: Harper & Row, 1988.